How mothers with postnatal depression create narcissism and psychopaths

Hans R Arnold

Copyright © 2013 Hans R Arnold
All rights reserved.

ISBN-10: 1492292540
ISBN-13: 9781492292548
Library of Congress Control Number: 2013916244
CreateSpace Independent Publishing Platform
North Charlston, South Carolina

Contents

Extensive Summary	1
Introduction To The General Theory	5
The Real Life Of The Narcissist	11
Terms And Definitions	15
Terms And Definitions I: Postnatal Depression	15
Terms And Definitions Ii: The Narcissistic Spectrum	18
How Hitler Became Hitler	23
Saddam Hussein	35
Internet Stalking And Narcissistic Behavior	39
Daniel Lynch Accid Attack Of Katie Piper	47
Ted Bundy, Serial Killer	51
Doctor Of Death	53
The Norway Shootings	57
The "Batman" Mass Shooting 2012	63
Boston Marathon Bombing 2013	65
Pablo Escobar: Billionaire Cocaine Dealer	69
The School Bully	75
Osama Bin Laden And Al-Qaeda	79
The Narcissist At Work	83
1938 Nazi Kristallnacht, Riots In London 2011 And Stockholm 2013	87
Goodwin, Rbs And The Profit Vacuum	89
The Failed Milgram Experiment	97
A New View: Psychologist Oliver Psychologist Oliver James	101
Arnoldology: Summary And Overview	105

Hans R Arnold

Appendix 1: Why Many Narcissistic And Psychopatic
"Twin Studies" Remain A Waste Of Time   115
Appendix 2 Case 5 - The Yorkshire Ripper   117
Appendix 3 Tv And Film Violence   119
Appendix 4- The Narcissistic Cowboy Builder   121
Short Summary   123

Extensive Summary

In this book Hans Arnold demonstrates how postnatal depression in the mother can create both narcissists and psychopaths. Using examples of famous serial killers and mass murderers, he demonstrates beyond reasonable doubt that, in each case, the mother's depression had a powerfully adverse effect on the child. For example, Hitler's mother lost two children to diphtheria 18 and 15 months before Adolf was born—and another died of measles when Adolf was only eight months. Hans Arnold analyzes Hitler's narcissism in the light of his mother's own suffering.

Put briefly, in order to get any emotional response at all from his mother Adolf developed a "narcissistic game" in order to shock his mother into at least some reaction, even if it was only an expression of despair. The youthful narcissist eventually became "hooked" on sensation, seeking more and more extreme reactions—not only from his mother or caregiver, but from whatever victim he could find. What was true for Adolf Hitler is unluckily also true for every child whose mother suffers from postnatal depression, even today.

It might start with making a milk glass fall, break and shatter into pieces, arousing a satisfying expression of shock from the mother. However, in order to arouse the same facial expression from a deeply depressed mother the child will over time need to escalate to far more horrendous deeds and by the age of three the child will be preoccupied with planning behaviour that will create the maximum expression of despair (n.b. the stronger the facial expression, the more narcissistic joy). The narcissist with little or no experience of love and compassion can become completely addicted to the game of creating the expression of despair in their "victims". After three years of age the budding narcissist is ready to try his or her skills on others, who on some level become nothing more than narcissistic prey.

We are all born selfish and narcissistic. As babies we cry when we are hungry, when we're cold or when we have a tummy-ache: we know nothing beyond ourselves and our own needs. Words like love, warmth, and compassion mean nothing to us. Instead these are things we learn from our mother or carer—unless they have postnatal depression and simply can't relate to us emotionally. In these cases the child simply doesn't learn to feel closeness, love or compassion. Sufferers from postnatal depression generally just sit there: deadened, still, apparently emotionless and unable to relate to the baby. It's impossible not to feel sorry for such women, and yet, without their assistance, the child not only can't learn what emotional interaction is. In its place the child can develop a lifelong addiction towards creating the strongest possible reaction (despair) in the expression of others. The stronger the expression the more narcissistic joy: it can become an addiction stronger than heroin, because it arises from the psyche. The narcissist has only one goal in life and that is, by any means, to create (and to feed off) the maximum despair in other peoples' faces.

On a larger scale we can see that events in Germany from 1914-1918 created an unprecedented number of mothers with postnatal depression: not only because of the war but also due to almost 3 million German deaths and a German revolt 1918-1919. Hyperinflation in the Weimar Republic 1918-1925 (with annual inflation up to 2 million percent) was yet another crushing burden. In November 1921 a single US dollar was worth 330 German Marks; while in November 1923 a single US dollar was worth 4,210,500,000,000 German Marks. For any mother needing to buy food for her family during this time the financial strain would have seemed unbearable and I suspect that most new mothers during this time would have ended up with postnatal depression.

And then, in 1929, the worldwide stockmarket crash sent Germany spiralling still deeper into depression and despair. Germany was (by far) the worst-hit country economically between 1914 and 1932, the period (not coincidentally) during which the generation was born that was to become the Nazi's strongest support base, simply because so many of their mothers suffered with postnatal depression. (It is only in a country as bruised as was Nazi Germany that somebody like Adolf Hitler can rise to power because possibly as many as 40% of the population might have become narcissistic.)

Using examples from history as well as serial killings as recent as Anders Breivik's Norway shootings, Arnold demonstrates how narcissism is behind events from Internet bullying to modern terrorism, opening up new perspectives on history, psychology, criminology, and corporate ethics. Using research by Dr Robert Hare (probably the world's foremost expert on narcissism) he elucidates how historical theory simply lacks the tools to explain how a nation of narcissists could take over a country like Nazi Germany.

Of course, the corporate world is a favored playground for narcissists, sociopaths and psychopaths and we need only recall companies including Enron, WorldCom, and Lehman Brothers to realize why. (We might also include individuals like Bernhard Madhoff, Sir Allen Stanford and Fred Goodwin.) There is almost nothing about the subject in management literature yet it remains one of the biggest reasons for corporate failure. Similarly, it's not every narcissist who commits a serious crime. It's often imagined that low social status or upbringing can lead to criminality, and yet Bernhard Madhoff (who swindled $65 billion) came from a boringly normal middle-class home. A home (and of course a mother or caregiver) can be poor but still loving and nurturing.

The same could be said about economics, where students ardently study interest rates, exports, imports and hundreds of other factors capable of impacting on a countries' growth—despite the fact that it only takes only a handful of people over-borrowing in order to neatly stitch up a country's economy for generations. In countries including Portugal, Italy, Greece, and Spain economic theory has come to a full stop, being replaced with a "Ponzi" economy where the politics of unlimited borrowing appear to defy every law of economics. From this it seems clear that, at least with regard to government economics, the temptation to borrow a fortune and to spend it on voters is hugely appealing for narcissists, on whom long-term consequences make little impact. Modern economics is impotent to handle huge government spending that one day in the future will indeed need to be repaid, yet we rarely read about narcissists or sociopaths in modern economic texts, despite their manifest influence.

Similarly in psychology there seems to be no theory regarding the damage that one person, such as a malignant narcissist, can do. Modern psychology appears to be far more interested in analyzing the illness, and then discussing how the patient feels about it all. Still less luckily, there's also another scenario, by no means uncommon, in which the psychotherapist or psychiatrist is themselves narcissistic, when, rather than helping, they cleverly push the bullied and/or damaged patient into madness. This can of course be very hard to prove because the therapist could simply say that the patient had an "underlying condition" that became manifest during therapy. (Sam Vatkin, self-confessed narcissist and psychotherapist is one of the few experts to talk openly on this subject.)

Using examples from school bullying to the Boston Marathon bombers, from Osama bin Laden to the Yorkshire Ripper, from Pablo Escobar to Fred Goodwin, Arnold makes connections never before attempted. After finishing this book you will understand that there is only one conflict in the world, the one between the narcissists and the rest of us.

This short but immensely ambitious book will alter your perspective forever.

Introduction To The General Theory

The second World War, Cambodia's killing fields, Saddam Hussain's Iraq, Muammar Gaddafi's Libya, the bank crash of 2008, Bernie Madhoff's "Ponzi" scheme, Enron, and the multiple debt crises of 2011 (Portugal, Italy, Ireland, Greece... the list goes on): these appear at first glance to be completely disparate events—to have nothing in common with each other. Yet, what if we were to find a common thread between them?

First: fewer than 1000 "movers and shakers" have been blamed for the 2008 financial crash. During the 2008 crash the guilty might have numbered fewer than 100, mainly finance ministers, along with leaders of the so-called "PIIGGS" (and other) countries. In the UK, Gordon Brown singlehandedly managed to build up a trillion pound debt, while in Italy most of the "credit" goes to Silvio Berlusconi. In America, Ronald Reagan laid a terrible foundation with "Reaganomics": reducing taxes while increasing military expenditure, and naturally the money to afford both will automatically rain down like manna from heaven!

Of course Reagonomics never worked, and the difference between fantasy and reality is the level of government borrowing to which every president since Reagan has added, not only the (Democratic) Obama, but both (Republican) Bushes with their horrific Iraq expenses. In fact, the destruction of any country's finances has much less to do with political ideology than with personal ego and the determination to pretend that governments alone are exempt from those economic laws that apply to the rest of us. (America's combined Iraq and Afghan war bill altogether has been estimated at 5 trillion by Nobel (economics) prizewinner George Stigler.)

In 2012-2013 Greece in particular made it amply clear to the rest of the world that political partying was fun as long as it lasted, but that the party's over, as civil servants, police, firemen, doctors, nurses, and schoolteachers went on strike while rioters attempted to wreck Athens. There isn't enough money in the country's coffers to pay the civil service, because Greece has frankly borrowed so much that only cash from Germany and the rest of the Eurozone is still keeping it afloat, with one emergency meeting after another to decide if the next payment to Greece will be the last.

Interestingly, Greece's debt has been consistently high since the 1980s, thanks to Andreas Papandreou and the PASOK Party (Panhellenic Socialist Movement) who enjoyed most of the power most of the time. To pretend that money can be conjured up like gold dust is nothing new in politics: conservative parties do it just as neatly as socialist ones. Yet it's still the hubris of individuals that created the debt crises of 2011: almost all of whom appeared far more concerned about their personal re-election than about the long-term future of their countries. One has to ask: how does economic theory handle the fact that we effectively have narcissists in power over most of the world?

Not well, is the answer: it being far easier to throw around variable concepts including interest rates, inflation-levels, and economic cycles instead of pointing out that narcissists in general lack any sense of reality.

To take a simple example: the common cold. It is easy to accept that a cold can cause different symptoms in different people. In those with better immune systems, a common cold is exactly that: just a common cold. The same cold can in those less fortunate deliver sinusitis, bronchitis or even pneumonia—can, in the worst-case scenario—even kill people. Many older people will die of a common cold because they have a weakened immune system and the germ is allowed to develop into pneumonia.

Having accepted this, it should come as no huge surprise that what psychiatrists refer to as an "antisocial personality" can manifest a wide array of damaging conditions, from narcissism, malignant narcissism or psychopathy (with narcissists on the lower end of the spectrum and psychopaths at the most extreme). A sociopath as bursar of a private school may do some harm, but a sociopath as chancellor of even a small country can ruin it.

New ideas and new thinking do not always come from expected places. Certain areas of science can tread water for decades or even centuries before a breakthrough occurs. Most of us are aware of the ancient Greeks' belief that the entire world is consisted of only four elements (earth, fire, water and air). This was part of received scientific wisdom for the better part of 2000 years. (It's not hard to see why, because when people make an urn they mix earth and water into clay, let it air-dry and finally harden it using fire.) Metals such as iron and gold also actually come from earth. Yet today if anyone attempted to explain chemistry as based only on the original "four elements" they would be ridiculed—and rightly. Nobody believes in the four elements anymore, although it was reckoned scientific truth for many hundreds of years. And yet, like Dmitri Mendeleev, the inventor of the system using the numbers of protons, electrons and neutrons for every known element as a basis for classification, I believe that we can use the narcissistic spectrum in order to analyse and categorize much of human behaviour.

Here I intend to demonstrate how much of human behavior has the same origins, in the first three years of a child's life. I hope to show that narcissism, sociopathy and psychopathy are the main culprits with regard to situations as apparently unrelated as corporate collapse, school bullying, dictatorships—even, in some cases, war.

Some years ago Mendeleev had a dream about neutrons, protons and electrons organising every element in the universe. This dream today dictates how chemistry is taught all over the world. Yet at CERN, the European Organization for Nuclear Research, scientists have recently found sixteen particles that must be classified in a new and different way, so—who knows—perhaps one day we will get a new periodic system based on something else?

I intend to show that Mendeleev's insight into neutrons, protons and electrons has a contemporary resonance with the connection between post-natal depression and the narcissistic spectrum. Just as one is a cornerstone of the physical world, the other is one of the cornerstones of society, generating narcissists, one after another, as well as explaining such otherwise inexplicable disasters as Hitler's persecution of the Jews, the 2008 world banking crisis, and so on.

We all know the chronological history of the WWII. This is not a book about when and where and how but rather about why such things happen. I could have chosen hundreds of examples, so when I selected Adolf Hitler and his life it is more a matter of familiarity and convenience than for any deeper reason.

Most people are aware how he and the Nazis took power in Germany, invaded Europe as well as the Soviet Union, while simultaneously perpetuating the horrors of the Holocaust. These are familiar from studying history, reading books, and watching TV series and films: WWII's "how, when and where" feature in school curricula all over the world. This is instead a book about "why" it happened and (although it might shock some people) how the seeds of the next World War and the next Adolf Hitler are germinating around us today, although naturally in different forms.

It will swiftly become apparent that Hitler's separation from reality during WWII has echoes in the economic crises of 2008 and 2011. We are generally far too willing to consider economic disasters as crises separate from the living people who caused them. If one steals a chocolate bar the police will chase you down the street, but if a banker or CEO steals millions of dollars quite often nothing happens—at least, not for years and years—sometimes never.

Similarly, many historians also suppose that the (harsh) peace treaty imposed upon Germany after WWI was to blame for WWII. No question: it ground an already spent Germany into the dirt. However, the treaty alone fails to make any sense whatsoever of the Holocaust. In fact, although I chose Hitler as my prime example, in all honesty I could have used Stalin or Mao or Saddam Hussein or Gaddafi just as well and almost as easily. It would not change the argument (the theory of postnatal depression in relation to narcissism, sociopathy and psychopathy) in the least.

This is the problem: We simply lack the tools to analyse evil. We can send astronauts to the moon; we can connect with people all over the world; we can demolish previously deathly illnesses with clever vaccines, but when it comes to evil we tend to look on helplessly, because we simply don't understand how people can "turn out" like that. Remember: during most of the twentieth century the social model was the recognised authority on how some people turn out to be "evil". Poverty, unemployment, domestic or sexual abuse have all been part of a social explanation that I personally believe (in 2013) to be obsolete. The worst part of the social explanation model is that it takes money and attention from the real problems while giving the glowing illusion that everything will turn out fine, as in some Disney fantasy.

Like Dmitri Mendeleev, who used the numbers of protons, electrons and neutrons in order to classify every known element, I believe that we can use the example of malignant narcissism in order to analyse and categorize a wide range of human behaviour. I hope to show that malignant narcissism, sociopathy and psychopathy is an underestimated, underrated and under-researched condition leading to untold amounts of human suffering.

As for evil: It's not hard to understand what evil looks like. Although philosophers have for centuries struggled to define it most people seem to have an answer when asked what it is. Adolf Hitler was evil: Josef Stalin and Saddam Hussein were evil and so was Mao. They are probably the best-known dictators, each of them responsible for millions of human deaths. But what about serial killers like Ted Bundy, Paul Bernardo, Clifford Olson and John Wayne Gacy—or Dr. Harold Shipman, who killed hundreds of his own patients? It's far from unreasonable to consider psychopaths, sociopaths, malignant narcissists and narcissists as merely the pointed tip of a Titanic-crushing iceberg.

The useful thing about Hitler as an example is that few historical figures are better documented. There are thousands of books about him personally, while his deeds and his genius at creating pure suffering are facts in history texts. I am one of the many who have always been intrigued by WWII: the causes of the war, the epic battles, the horrors of the Holocaust and the ultimate defeat of Nazi Germany. But my intention here is not to "explain" Nazism, which probably had a thousand roots but is now mostly over, but is instead to elucidate malignant narcissism, which remains all too alive and well in 2013. Nazism did not exactly end with Adolf Hitler: there remain a tiny but stubborn rump of people who espouse it. However narcissism continues to absolutely thrive, because there are millions of mothers still suffering postnatal depression throughout the world today.

The Real Life Of The Narcissist

During a conference at the University of Mons, Belgium, a young woman asked Professor Robert Hare if a psychopath could be cured with psychotherapy. The Professor considered, and then asked in return, "Can a cat stop being a cat?"

In short, in a world that Professor Hare knows all too well as a Canadian-based prison psychologist, almost every prisoner in more secure prison units might be categorised as narcissists, sociopaths or psychopaths. (In the general population he estimates that 5% might be narcissists, 4% sociopaths and 1% psychopaths.) It is almost impossible to open up a book in psychiatry or psychology relating to psychopaths that doesn't reference Professor Hare as a world-leading expert in the subject.

"Can a cat stop being a cat?" Professor Hare asked, and proceeded to explain that a cat's nature is to chase and catch mice, sometimes playing with them before the kill. In the real world around 10% are cats (narcissists, sociopaths or psychopaths) while the rest of us are just simply mice (or their victims, in Professor Hare's analogy).

Professor Hare further explained on that occasion that psychotherapy will probably have no effect on a psychopath, due to his intrinsic nature. But not even Professor Hare could explain exactly how narcissists and sociopaths are created, other than suggesting "environmental factors" (in the case of psychopaths, combined "environmental factors" and genes). What environmental factors he might be referring to have never been clarified, until now.

My own "Eureka moment" came when I watched a TV programme about two mothers with postnatal depression (Channel 4: "Help me love my baby",

2007). It was immediately clear that neither mother could relate emotionally to their child: there was no eye contact between them whatsoever. Babies imitate their mother's movements and facial expressions and if the mother has the blank and lifeless expression of a deeply depressed person than the baby will adapt, yet still there will remain a deep-seated craving to establish <u>any</u> form of human contact with the mother. Sooner or later an accident will occur (like a broken milk glass) causing the mother to unmistakably register some emotion—and because it's the first time in the baby's life the moment will be one of indescribable joy for the baby. From that moment the baby will be as "hooked" as a heroin addict on creating "accidents" in order to enjoy the mother's reaction. This I believe to be the root cause of narcissism, sociopaths and psychopathy or in Professor Hare's words, "How a cat becomes a cat".

When I saw Dr Sue Lamb's documentary the idea suddenly struck me that this might have happened to Adolf Hitler's mother when he was a baby. I researched thoroughly to see if there was something in his mother's life that could have given her postnatal depression and it did not take long to discover that Klara Hitler suffered no fewer than two extant children dying (from diphtheria) only months before Adolf was born. She also lost a third child to measles when Adolf was eight months old.

For me, this was a light-bulb moment. This was the moment when I first recognised how Adolf Hitler became what he became. It would have been strange indeed had his mother not suffered with deep, deep postnatal depression, causing the infant Adolf to simply become addicted to causing her to express shock, horror and despair. (The stronger the facial expression, the bigger the narcissistic "kick" given to the youthful narcissist.) This I believe is the core drive behind narcissism, sociopathy and psychopathy: to inflict as much as possible shock, horror and despair in the victims' faces as possible. The more reaction, the more narcissistic joy.

To recapitulate: two things happen to the baby whose mother suffers postnatal depression. The first is that there is an almost complete lack of emotional bonding between mother and baby (worse still, there is evidence to suggest that, if one can't learn to bond before the age of three than one probably will never be able to). Those brain connections that fail to develop during the first three years have missed their only chance to exist.

The second thing that happens is that the baby develops a lifelong way of thinking regarding the best ways to create maximum negative emotional impact on others: their victims, in short. To put it in Professor Hare's terminology, the cat learns to manipulate, chase, catch, play with and sometimes murder mice, if not always on a Nazi-like scale.

Although this has never been written about before to my knowledge, my own theory is as follows:

1) Postnatal depression involving mothers who can't emotionally relate to their baby might be responsible for 85% of the instances of narcissism and psychopathy (the narcissistic spectrum).

2) Sheer neglect from mothers might supply 10%: mothers who, for different reasons, deny the baby emotionally because she is simply not very interested, for whatever reason.

3) Narcissistic mothers who themselves find it impossible to emotionally relate to anybody (including their own baby) probably account for around 5% of the incidence of narcissism and psychopathy.

I should stress that the figures above are simply estimates, based on Professor Hare's original figures. However any damage will occur in a baby before the age of three. If a baby fails to learn to emotionally relate to its mother or alternative caregiver before the age of three then it is unlikely that the baby will not be able to relate to anybody emotionally for the rest of their life. The brain connections will have missed their only chance to be formed, and the narcissist will be obliged to cope with life the best they can as a narcissist (while pretending that they care for other people like anybody else, even if the reality is that they cannot).

It does not take a Ph.D. in psychology to understand this and it is even easier to see how one mother with three children can emotionally relate wonderfully to the first three—but, when they are all taken from her by illness, with the fourth child postnatal depression sets in and she has insufficient emotional strength left to relate to her new baby. It is only speculation, if fascinating speculation, but who knows what might have happened—or not happened—had Hitler's three dead siblings lived?

Terms And Definitions

TERMS AND DEFINITIONS I: POSTNATAL DEPRESSION

It is obvious that postnatal depression has always been part of the female experience, though often going unrecognised. This illness can hit the maternal psyche terribly, making mothers feel deeply depressed, entirely lacking in emotional energy, unable to concentrate, and (in the worst cases) even antagonistic to their new baby. In terms of research, some of the most fascinating studies suggest that women in conflict zones (such as Palestine, North Korea etc.) are likeliest to suffer, due to preexisting factors linked to normal depression, while in the developed world poverty, divorce and lack of family or partner's sympathy and support are the main contributory factors. (However, it's important to note that any woman can get postnatal depression through hormonal malfunctions alone.)

Sometimes for no obvious reason the mother can be affected, shutting down emotionally, and finding it difficult to relate to her newborn (the core of postnatal depression is the inability to relate to the baby emotionally). Typically, the mother can just about feed her baby and change the nappies, and that's about it. Otherwise she will sit and stare out through the window (or even at a wall) for hours: unable to think, enjoy life or even to communicate with others, especially with her newborn. The deeply depressed mother is unlikely to kiss, cuddle, hold or talk to the baby. Depression can grip to such an extent that the mother will even avoid eye contact with the baby.

It's impossible to over-emphasize the importance of eye contact, both to a newborn and to my theory of Malignant Narcissism. Deprivation in the earliest days and years can impact hugely on human behaviour.

How common is it? The Royal College of Psychiatrists estimates that between 10% and 15% of British mothers suffer postnatal depression, although the severity of the condition varies widely. The percentage seeking help in places like the Anna Freud clinic in London is, from a statistical point of view, negligible, despite the fact that treatment is purely focused on the mother's recovery. And astonishingly, at least to my knowledge, no studies have yet been done connecting mothers with postnatal depression and their children's future prospects.

The incidence of postnatal depression—in addition to being only variably recognised—also seems to vary from country to country depending on war, conflicts, economic factors, and hardships in general. It would be easy to conclude that poor countries endure a higher degree of postnatal as well as many other depressive states, but bereavement, financial crashes, and generalized depression itself are common conditions worldwide, while some causes of depression are believed to be hormonal.

Probably postnatal depression's biggest impact in terms of popular culture was with the publication of Down Came the Rain: A Mother's Story of Depression and Recovery, by Brooke Shields. This well-known actress had for some years longed for a baby, yet still the actual experience of motherhood hit her like a sledgehammer. Perhaps her parents' divorce, her father's recent death or natural fears about maintaining her career might have been contributory factors, but Shields' postnatal experience still represents that of a great swathe of well-off women living in developed countries.

In short, whether the new mother is as rich as Shields or as intensely deprived as a single Somali mother of eight, they are in the same emotionally bankrupt state if they can't feel emotionally attached to their child. The most approachable programme on the subject in my own experience was Channel 4's "Help Me Love My Baby": a two-part documentary about how two mothers coped (when they couldn't).

The first mother, for example, felt fear, anger and even hatred towards her daughter, Issy. Both mother and daughter avoided any eye contact: it looked almost like some bizarre dance. The second programme showcased Sophie, a mother with twin daughters who couldn't relate to one of them, Gracie.

The second case study seems to me the more fascinating, as well as having more relevance to identical twin studies. In my opinion psychologically-based twin studies later in life may not sufficiently take into account the possibility that—literally from birth—a mother of twins might feel emotionally more distant from one twin than from the other. Of course, such information is by its very nature hard to come by—not only because of the length of time involved, perhaps twenty of forty years after the birth, but because any mother concerned is often unwilling either to admit or to discuss it. (See Appendix 1.)

Nor do the police necessarily pay sufficient attention to the possibility of psychopathic behaviour as directly resulting from postnatal depression. For example, not long ago there was a mass shooting in Britain, where a man shot his twin brother, and then followed up this murder by killing eleven other people all over Cumbria. It's not hard to understand how his mother's long-past postnatal depression could have laid the foundation for the tragedy, yet such will probably be the last factor the police investigation would consider. There has simply not been enough research done about the connection between a mother's postnatal depression and her offspring's crimes, committed perhaps decades later!

For the same reason I firmly believe that criminologists are far too likely to consider abusive families or social deprivation as precipitating factors for crime, simply because such potential factors are far easier to research than the mother's possible post-natal depression. (In addition, criminals often boast a long and temptingly well-documented crime record, much easier to research.)

As Melanie Klein discovered, babies always mimic their mothers or original caregivers, with the attachment period being particularly critical. Because babies are expected to cry, their depressive crying is often overlooked. A baby born to a mother with postnatal depression will miss the emotional bonding and even the brain development necessary for empathy. At the earliest age, the child's brain grows very fast, with new brain cells and connections created at amazing speed. Occasionally specialists examine the brain waves of sociopaths or psychopaths, finding evidence of stunted development to this frontal lobe or that section. This is only to be expected in the context of the emotional deprivation so typical of postnatal depression.

Hans R Arnold

TERMS AND DEFINITIONS II: THE NARCISSISTIC SPECTRUM

Terminology can be a bugbear, yet in the interests of clarity we need to establish our terms. It's pointless attempting to discuss postnatal depression as a cause of narcissism without at least some attempt to define narcissism and its extreme form, psychopathy.

The narcissistic spectrum involves everything from the narcissist to the malignant narcissist to the psychopath, although the borders between the categories are fuzzy, to say the least. Dictators and serial killers are—in every sense—the "extremes" of the spectrum, but that makes it no easier to differentiate between malignant narcissists, sociopaths and psychopaths. There can be no clear definitions here, because various behaviours overlap and if we list ten characteristics for each we might observe that as many as eight might be the same. In addition narcissism has given way to other terms in recent times.

The Diagnostic and Statistical Manual of Mental Disorders (of which the current edition is commonly referred to as DSM-5) describes mainly the symptoms of narcissism but does not explain how and why it is created. (Indeed, recently the words narcissism and psychopathy have been replaced with "Antisocial Behavior".) The problems with DSM definitions are that psychiatrists are in charge of it. We have no way of ascertaining the numbers of narcissists etc. in such professions, but I can't think it unfair to assume that it is high. (Sam Vaknin, a self-confessed narcissist and psychiatrist who writes brilliantly on narcissism can't be alone, even if few other psychiatrists are prepared to be honest about it. It is after all a narcissistic trait to lie.)

However, it's worth looking at the list of narcissistic symptoms the DSM last published:

1) obvious self-focus in interpersonal exchanges
2) problems in sustaining satisfying relationships
3) lack of psychological awareness
4) difficulty with empathy
5) problems distinguishing self from others
6) hypersensitivity to any insults (or imagined insults)
7) vulnerability to shame rather than guilt

8) haughty body language
9) flattery towards people who admire and affirm them
10) detestation of those who fail to admire them
11) use of others without considering the cost to them
12) pretending to more importance than they truly have
13) bragging and exaggerating their own achievements
14) claiming to be "expert" at many things
15) inability to view the world from the perspective of other people
16) denial of remorse and absence of gratitude

These can be compared and contrasted with the definition of psychopath:

1) glibness/superficial charm
2) grandiose sense of self-worth
3) pathological lying
4) manipulative behaviour
5) lack of remorse or guilt
6) emotional shallowness
7) callousness, lack of empathy
8) failure to accept responsibility for own actions
9) constant need for stimulation
10) parasitic lifestyle
11) lack of realistic long-term goals
12) impulsiveness
13) irresponsibility
14) poor behavioural controls
15) early behavioural problems (juvenile delinquency)
16) revocation of conditional release
17) criminal versatility
18) numerous short-term marital relationships
19) promiscuous sexual behavior

The point here is obvious: when compared side by side one can barely spot the difference between narcissism and psychopathy: the differences are mainly academic. This makes it confusing for normal people to understand, which is incidentally my point. As I see it, a narcissist is someone whose mother almost certainly had postnatal depression and who thus is unable to relate to others emotionally; while a sociopath is a narcissist with more accomplished social skills who is mainly interested in garnering money. A psychopath shares many qualities with the narcissist or sociopath but—according to Robert Hare—this condition might have at least some genetic component.

As Professor Hare succinctly puts it:

"This PCL-R (see graph below) is referred to by some as the "gold standard" in terms of assessing psychopathy. (n.b. High PCL-R scores are positively associated with measures of impulsivity and aggression, Machiavellianism, and persistent criminal behavior. At the same time they arenegatively associated with measures of empathy and affiliation.)

"Thirty out of a maximum score of forty is recommended as the cut-off point for the psychopath, although there is little scientific support for this, while for research purposes a cut-off score of 25 is sometimes used... PCL-R items were always designed to be split in two. Factor 1 involves interpersonal or affective (emotion) personality traits, with higher values associated with narcissism with and low empathy as well as social dominance and less fear or depression.

"By contrast Factor 2 involves either impulsive-irresponsible or antisocial behaviors and is associated with a maladaptive lifestyle (including criminality). These two factors correlate to some extent. Each factor is sometimes further subdivided into two (interpersonal vs affect items for Factor 1, and impulsive-irresponsible lifestyle vs antisocial behavior items for Factor 2). "Promiscuous sexual behavior" and "many short-term marital relationships" have sometimes been left out in such divisions." (Hare, 2003).

Psychopathy Checklist-Revised: Factors, Facets, and Items[5]		
Factor 1	Factor 2	Other items
Facet 1: Interpersonal · glibness/ superficial charm · grandiose sense of self-worth · <u>pathological lying</u> · cunning/ manipulative · lack of remorse or guilt · emotionally shallow · lack of empathy · failure to accept responsibility for own actions	Facet 3: Lifestyle · need for stimulation/proneness to boredom · parasitic lifestyle · lack of realistic, long-term goals · <u>impulsiveness</u> · irresponsibility Facet 4: Antisocial · poor behavioral controls · early behavioral problems · <u>juvenile delinquency</u> · revocation of conditional release · criminal versatility	· many short-term marital relationships · <u>promiscuous</u> sexual behavior

In short, psychologists remain far from agreed on exactly what a narcissist, sociopath or psychopath is, and where the borderline falls between them. There is a form of narcissism (called malignant narcissism) that psychologists including Sam Vaknin maintain is the same as psychopathy. Professor Robert Hare suggests that psychologists consider the same condition narcissism that sociologists term sociopathy. However, for the purposes of this book it is unimportant precisely where the boundaries fall.

It makes no difference to a farmer if it was a mere storm that destroyed his crops or if people from the meteorological office term the storm a hailstorm, twister, tornado, thunderstorm, dust storm, blizzard, squall or gale. The same thing can be said about the victims of narcissists, sociopaths or psychopaths, whether targeted through school bullying, work misery, financial fraud or even murder. It's small consolation to be told that the deed was done by a narcissist, a sociopath or a psychopath. To give something a Latin name serves no purpose for a victim, though the same victim might take some meagre comfort in learning that they themselves were not to blame or that, as Professor Hare puts it, a cat is a cat in a world of mice. (Or, then again, they might not.)

One day we might learn to recognise narcissistic behavior for what it is: it might even become common to detect it. And yet such people are attracted to positions of power, which makes it harder to cope with them, even once the situation becomes clear. Also, there are clearly a range of professional occupations that narcissists are unsuited for yet still survive in—simply because it gives them their best opportunities to manipulate people.

The term "narcissistic spectrum" is often used to describe anyone from the low-level narcissist all the way up to the truly malignant narcissist (even psychopath), in that there are mainly shades of difference between them. I believe there to be a common factor but it's hard to investigate some forty years later. When a serial killer is caught the last thing investigating detectives or criminologists ask is if the killer's mother suffered postnatal depression thirty, forty, even fifty years before! It can be almost impossible to establish, although I would like to see a nationwide investigation of the link between postnatal depression and such illnesses as narcissism, sociopathy, psychopathy, even including the autistic spectrum (when despite every effort of the mother the individual can still find it difficult to relate to others).

But let's start with a classic case: Adolf Hitler.

How Hitler Became Hitler

Erich Fromm first coined the term "malignant narcissism" in 1964. A brilliant Jewish psychiatrist, he was possibly the first to understand that Hitler failed to fit the normal description of psychopath. (For example, a psychopath is generally reckoned to be a murderer, but—at least to my knowledge—Hitler did not personally kill anybody.) This may sound finicky, given the truth about the Holocaust, but it's still an important psychological distinction to make: Adolf Hitler gave orders for people to be put to death, but personally he did not shoot, hang or gas anybody.

As mentioned previously there remains confusion today—even among psychiatric experts—regarding terms like malignant narcissists, sociopaths and psychopaths, and DSM-5 (the most recent psychiatric book of definitions) fails to bring any clarity to the subject. This is probably because the Diagnostic and Statistical Manual of Mental Disorder was mainly written by pharmaceutical companies, whose guiding principle is that only those mental disorders curable by prescriptions rate as an illness. Therefore, because malignant narcissists, sociopaths and psychopaths cannot be cured by medicine, all are shoved under the all-singing, all-dancing category of Antisocial Personality Disorders. Thus if you deliberately break societal laws, you can be neatly classified as having Antisocial Personality Disorder. This way—almost literally—lies madness.

Similarly, it's easy to see how somebody deliberately smashing shop windows in order to steal could be classified as having Antisocial Personality Disorder. However, in Nazi Germany during the Kristallnacht in 1938 it had been made legal to burn Jewish synagogues and demolish Jewish shops. Therefore, bizarrely enough, under the DSM-4 definition of Antisocial Personality Disorder, what occurred during Kristallnacht would <u>not</u> be classified as antisocial behaviour, despite the fact that Adolf Hitler himself, according to the same terminology, would have suffered from an Antisocial Personality Disorder!

Modern psychiatry has still not figured out what kind of man Adolf Hitler was. Having read every book I could get hold of regarding WWII I always wondered. We know from numerous books and films and documentaries as much as can be known about how and when. But my question was always why? (The recognised answer was always: he was a psychopath.) We can all imagine what a psychopath is like. But what kind of a psychopath fails to kill people?

Erich Fromm realised this when he coined the expression malignant narcissism, describing in great details those characteristics required to be considered a malignant narcissist. But how are such narcissists born? DNA? If Adolf Hitler had "evil" DNA, then surely his siblings would also have been evil. But the evidence is that nobody in his family bore any relation to Hitler: in fact, his only surviving brother moved to the UK after WWI and fought gallantly against the Nazis in WWII. Assuming that Hitler's brother too was caned as a child—not an uncommon punishment in Germany in the early twentieth century—it didn't turn him into a violent narcissist. There must be more to malignant narcissism—and more to Hitler.

In this chapter I will attempt to prove why Adolf Hitler became what he became—though the theory is in no way constructed "simply" to explain the character of Adolf Hitler. The theory might be easy to understand, but its implications are many.

Adolf Hitler's mother Klara was, according to her doctor, a "very quiet, sweet, affectionate" person. Photos show a young woman with clear pale eyes, a conscientious mouth and a perfect complexion. Her children adored her (apparently Hitler was grief-stricken when she died.) Certainly her husband, Alois Hitler, appeared ill-suited to her: much older and twice married before, he was apparently a womanizer who spent much of his time in the tavern, when not working as a customs officer. Neighbours recalled that he was prone to "shout continuously" at his many children, Adolf among them. Photographs display a plump, self-satisfied face with piggy eyes and a thin mouth accentuated by a flourishing mustache.

Klara was his third wife, very much his junior, and it's hard to imagine she enjoyed it much, despite her conscientious Catholicism. As mentioned previously, just before and immediately after Adolf's birth Klara lost three of her other children: surely ample excuse for postnatal depression even without an unsympathetic, demanding husband! (It has often been surmised that Alois's brutality shaped Hitler's own mindset, something that I personally doubt. However, I do suspect that Alois's boorish behaviour—arriving home probably expecting instant attention, food and sex—doubtless exacerbated Klara's likely postnatal depression.)

And it's certainly easy enough to imagine Klara, still deep in mourning for her dead children, almost unable to cope with the weight of her anguish, being unable to respond to (or even to meet) Adolf's infant gaze—perhaps being even afraid to meet it, to make the connection, lest this child too be wrenched away from her by death.

It's also easy to imagine the young Adolf, initially puzzled and rebuffed, not connecting with his mother emotionally, his frontal brain simply not making—in the first critical years—those crucial connections that allow empathy and humanity to link up. The young Hitler may have been condemned by circumstance to narcissism and to the inability to relate (emotionally) to anyone. In short, nurture—or, to be more precise, the lack of nurture—translates to, or even becomes, human nature by default.

We are all born narcissists: it's part of the human condition. We're all at first cosseted in a warm and cosy womb; therefore, to be born is to come out into a cold, uncomfortable world where we only have attention sufficient for our personal needs. (In fact, to the baby, only he counts!) Like a blank sheet of paper we await input, feedback, encouragement and warmth from our mothers or replacement caregivers. If we fail to receive these, due to postnatal depression or for any other reason, than true narcissism takes root, like a particularly aggressive weed, stultifying and arresting normal psychological development. (Grown-up narcissists can often have tantrums like three-year-olds: there are hints of these in some of Hitler's rage-filled speeches.)

So there was nothing special about Adolf Hitler's situation. He was just a narcissist with a mother who I suspect loved him but who—in the most crucial period of his life—almost certainly couldn't share either love or even eye contact with her child. She probably almost always looked away from him, causing Adolf to become absolutely hooked on creating powerful reactions in other people, whose strongest expression is despair. In short, when the adult Adolf was able to create deeply emotional expressions in other peoples' faces he was in narcissistic heaven. Then all he had left to wish for was to find like-minded people, who also relished the most extreme examples of emotional despair.

I contend that most of the vitriolic hatred Hitler aimed at Jews, Communists, homosexuals etc. was nothing more or less than a huge narcissistic cover-up for what he craved: to bathe, to luxuriate, in the strongest possible expressions of others' anguish. This was the facial expression that he learned to strive for as a baby, when his brain became hard-wired for sensation until he became <u>physically incapable</u> of feeling real compassion for others. There's no therapeutic psychoanalysis in the world that can touch—let alone deal with—a lack as deep as this. It is nurture's ultimate victory over nature: Hitler became addicted to despair as a heroin addict is addicted to heroin (or in his case morphine) since Adolf Hitler for many years injected morphine. They were mostly morphine addicts at the top of the Nazi party, including Goering and Himmler, possibly since morphine makes it easier to cope with unreality, though completely unrelated to their narcissism.

Now that we have come to even vaguely understand a case as extreme as Adolf Hitler's, we may be better equipped to observe how narcissistic people have shaped our life and pasts. We may suspect what their true aim is but still underestimate how skilful they might be at covering it up with something seemingly completely different.

The best example of this I ever heard of was Rudolf Hess, who flew to Scotland in 1942 (with, I feel confident, Adolf Hitler's blessing, since he was very close to Hitler) in order to try to persuade the British to join the Nazis because they supposedly had "no chance" of winning the war.

At the Nuremberg trial Hess came up with the surreal explanation that Jews had "hypnotised" Adolf Hitler into killing them in order to ruin the Nazis' reputation. Thus even at the summation of the war the supposed Jewish conspiracy was alive and well in the Nazi camp! (Shall we call this "narcissistic logic?"—in other words, the type of impossible logic entirely invented, ready to be used as an excuse whenever needed, however ridiculous it might appear to normal people.)

But naturally there are other narcissists besides top Nazis. We can see a similar pattern in Saddam Hussein, whose father abandoned his mother six months before his birth, leaving the family in great financial hardship. Even worse, at least in terms of probable maternal depression, shortly after Saddam was born his thirteen-year-old brother succumbed to cancer. For his poor mother, all the precipitating factors were in place: financial hardship, personal betrayal and the loss of a child. I have no doubt that Saddam's horrific level of narcissism sprang from his mother's postnatal depression (see the following chapter).

Similar traumas may be observed in the childhood of Joseph Stalin, whose mother lost no fewer than <u>four</u> other children to various illnesses. Nor can it be pure coincidence that Mao Zedong's mother lost two other children during his childhood (she was apparently married to a very brutal man as well).

The list goes on. Hemilda Escobar, mother of Pablo Escobar, the Columbian billionaire drug lord, was held siege by bandits when Pablo was still a baby. At one point the family was forced to barricade themselves in their country house, while burning, looting and killing happened just outside. Even Osama bin Laden, born in the lap of luxury as the son of a Saudi Arabian billionaire, was undoubtedly influenced by his mother's misery, as her husband chose to divorce her and then to shun her shortly after Osama bin Laden was born. It's hard to imagine any mother escaping postnatal depression under such circumstances. (There is very little a Muslim woman can do, if her husband decides to divorce her. In an Islamic society her rights are few.)

Indeed I believe that I safely can say that if you can show me a narcissist then I can demonstrate either a mother with postnatal depression or a narcissistic mother capable of grossly ignoring her baby before the age of three. Events later on in life merely act as catalysts, accelerating or exacerbating the progress of the already existing condition.

Interestingly, in the 1978 film <u>The Boys From Brasil</u> Dr Josef Mengele tries through cloning to recreate 94 boys with Adolf Hitler's DNA. The plan was to place them in various environments around the world, each with a forty-two-year-old "mother" and a civil-servant "father" and then to kill the "father" once the Hitler clones reached thirteen. Knowing what we now today this would not have made the cloned Hitlers, DNA or no DNA, into the narcissistic monster the true Hitler became. (In fact, the fake fathers might just as well have been spared: it would have to have been luckless "siblings" who would have been assassinated, in order to propel the "mothers" into the kind of torment Klara Hitler suffered.)

Which leads us to the "narcissistic game": one not in any way unique to Adolf Hitler, but instead completely natural to any narcissist, old or young.

Let's imagine little Adolf sitting in a baby chair and being fed by his mother with a tiny spoon (she feeling deeply depressed, possibly even suicidal). One day, perhaps accidentally, perhaps out of sheer boredom, he spills the milk on to the floor, provoking an expression of despair in his mother (perhaps because of the waste, perhaps because she had no more milk in the house, perhaps simply because of her already overburdened heart). This facial expression—caused in the first instance by accident—would have fascinated the baby, entranced by his own power to produce it. From that moment young Adolf would be "hooked" on creating that expression of despair in his mother's face. More milk bottles might be pulled over, more glasses would surely be broken, not to mention precious porcelain "accidentally" smashed onto the floor (the possibilities of creating anguish in a mother's face are almost endless.)

So while normal children will laugh with their mother (and father), be tickled and talked to, kissed, hugged, and cuddled while their brain connections explode with growth during the first three years, in Hitler's childhood almost none of this occurred, and thereby young Adolf (by the age of three) became instead a precocious player of the narcissistic game. For Hitler, and indeed any narcissist, the exhilaration of causing misery becomes part of their brain's "hard-wiring" until they become as dependent upon reveling in despair as a normal non-narcissist might be of feeling warmed by expressions of love and kindness.

Thus any debate referencing nurture vs nature is of no importance. In this instance, at least, nurture <u>creates</u> nature: or, in other words, nurture creates the brain cells and connections (or the lack thereof) meaning that by Adolf Hitler's fourth birthday he was probably already on the hunt for new prey for his narcissistic game, beyond his vanquished mother. And his first ancillary victim was probably his father, Alois Hitler.

It is likely (though unproven) that Adolf Hitler set fire to his father's beloved beehives at least once. I can imagine Alois coming home one day from work, only to see his beehive—fruit of long and patient effort—razed to the ground. Whether or not it was really Adolf's fault, his famously short-tempered father might well have beaten his son for it.

Later perhaps Adolf learns slyness, perhaps he manages to set fire to the beehive with his father nearby, so he can from the safety of his bedroom enjoy a ringside view of his father's despair while attempting in vain to rescue his beloved beehive. Many people at this might imagine that the arsonist's joy is simply in seeing the heat, ash, dust, the aspiring flames scorching upwards. Instead it's the fear and despair of his victims that thrills the narcissistic arsonist. From a young age Adolf Hitler was apparently adept at arson and his father's emotional reaction while failing to put out the flames was so delightful to him that no amount of beating could prevent him seeking out such ecstasy again.

Both psychologists and historians have suggested that Adolf Hitler and his siblings were fiercely bullied by his father until his death (when Adolf was 13) and that somehow Adolf's impotent rage against his father became projected towards others, including the Jews. This I believe is a Freudian theory and as obsolete as Freud himself: because, although beating children in the late 1800s and early 1900s was common, I suspect that Alois Hitler was a victim of his narcissistic son rather than other way around.

Adolf Hitler became who he became because of his mother Klara's deep-seated postnatal depression. His father's bad temper probably only had an indirect effect, as a catalyst, because he was unable or unwilling to emotionally support his wife. Probably Alois's influence on what Adolf Hitler was marginal compared to his wife's utter withdrawal and depression.

We don't need to imagine Adolf Hitler's love for shock, horror and despair in people's faces. We can see it in the archive film of when the Reichstag in Berlin was set on fire (27 February 1933), which was thoroughly filmed from all angles, not excepting ordinary Germans' stunned misery. (The Nazis had forced a Jew to light the fire and during the—also recorded—trial the Nazi judge declared it "irrelevant" that the Jew had a gun to his head when this took place, and judged him responsible.)

Of course, with the torching of the Berlin Parliament the last hope of democracy shriveled to ashes. The Nazis could then do whatever they liked in Germany—and they did.

In the same fashion, archive film amply manifests the Czechs' despair when the Nazis invaded Czechoslovakia—though it was particularly movingly demonstrated the face of the then-Czechoslovakian President Edvard Benes. He was secretly filmed—a telling detail—during his meeting with Adolf Hitler (5 September 1938) when he was given an ultimatum: cooperate or be invaded. (His shocked reaction can still be seen on YouTube).

Hans R Arnold

Not to mention how Hitler reacted to the famous 20 July 1944 assassination attempt—rendered in the film <u>Operation Valkyrie.</u> (Each plotter was was executed and filmed, for Hitler's amusement. They were hanged by piano wire, in order to lengthen their agony, including Claus Von Stauffenberg, who placed the bomb.) Adolf Hitler clearly had a deep-seated satisfaction in watching fear and suffering, a trait I believe central to truly understanding not only Hitler personally, but also the Nazis in general and narcissism in particular. To understand the narcissist's thrill at watching their victim's anguish is to get a deeper understanding of what the narcissist is and most of all what creates the narcissist.

Five thousand people were executed in Nazi Germany after that assassination attempt, with some of the executions filmed so that Hitler could gloat over them. There are no records as to how often Hitler watched such tapes, and only a few of the films survive. However I firmly believe that Hitler would have viewed in great detail and with great narcissistic pleasure not only such executions but even the gassings of people in concentration camps. (This may even be one reason for such camps' very existence: for Hitler's sick pleasure in viewing other's despair.)

All this may be hard for normal people to grasp, but for a narcissist it makes perfect sense. Since Hitler's personal guards (the SS) controlled every concentration camp around Europe Hitler could easily have requested films of executions or gassings: the SS would have been more than happy to comply.

It is unsurprising to me that in the last few days in the bunker it was Joseph Goebbels and his family who stayed and died with Hitler and Eva Braun. I believe that Goebbels shared a special bond with Hitler through their taste for "snuff films". This is not a normal taste in any respect and I believe most historians have missed this crucial point. Indeed I believe it possible that watching private "snuff films" from around Europe was a critical personal motivation for Adolf Hitler and the Nazis to invade the rest of Europe in the first place.

In Hitler's private night cinema audience there would have been Joseph Goebbels (behind the film projector), Heinrich Himmler (the SS chief), Hermann Wilhelm Goering of the Air Force, Hitler's private secretary Martin Bormann and also Reinhard Heinrich (concentration camps). Perhaps Adolf Eichmann (transport to the camps) might have been included. But this private cinema of Hitler's was really for a tiny exclusive group of specially trusted narcissists and, in that light, their deeds make some kind of twisted sense. We can see that there

How mothers with postnatal depression...

was something the top Nazis craved far more than gold: probably the most grotesque and horrific "snuff film" material the world has seen.

For the approximately 90% of us who are not narcissistic (Professor Hare's estimate) it is utterly unimaginable that such things happen. But they did happen and—to a lesser extent—still happen even today where narcissists enjoy "happy slapping" on YouTube, and share appalling assaults on iphones, where watching the despair of others counts as joy. In this respect the leading Nazis were just average narcissists, doing what narcissists normally do (if not normally on such an unspeakable scale) while using "narcissistic logic" to justify their actions, even to the extent of killing communists and Jews for the "good" of humanity.

They would have eaten a good vegetarian alcohol-free dinner (because Hitler was a vegetarian teetotaller) and after dinner they would have gone in to Hitler's private cinema to watch an entertaining film, together with the ladies. However, after midnight the ladies would retire, and "snuff films" would be shown to the selected and trusty audience under the watchful eye of Joseph Goebbels (who also guarded the most appalling of the films). Most of these, I feel confident, were burned, because film burns very well, leaving almost no trace. And although it can't now be proved, I also believe that this constituted a personal motivation for Hitler to set up concentration camps all over Europe.

It's clear that watching films of invasions and executions (and—probably— of concentration camps) was Adolf Hitler's favorite pastime, and although historians have not found films made from inside gas chambers, I believe that they were made. However, rather than seeing the Nazis as some kind of bizarre aberration I firmly believe that understanding the source of narcissism in Hitler will help us to understand the roots of narcissism itself, because Hitler's unlucky mother was neither the first nor the last woman to suffer from deep-seated postnatal depression, and for that reason unable to relate to her baby.

And so a picture emerges whereby Adolf Hitler and the Nazis seamlessly move from attacking German communists to attacking socialists and intellectuals. Not until the infamous "Kristallnacht" (9 November 1938) did they truly turn on the Jews. I believe that the invasion of Poland (1 September 1939) was mainly because they were running out of victims internally: they were sourcing fresh narcissistic prey. (Fascinatingly, the invasion of Poland was filmed and shown to Hitler.)

Indeed, if one was German and an accomplished narcissist in the 1930s, the Nazi Party must have held considerable appeal. There must of course have been very many who joined the Nazi party for other—even for purely political or overtly nationalistic—reasons. But if we look back to the Germany just after WWI, recalling how many wives and would-be wives had lost their husbands in battle, remembering inflation on a level unmatched before or since, there is little doubt that depression (not only postnatal depression) was certain to be prevalent. Of course, in the Soviet Union, France, Britain and many other places terrifying numbers of young men were also lost. Yet only in Germany was there the 'perfect storm' of millions of lost young men, eye-watering levels of hyperinflation—and, of course, defeat.

It's sometimes forgotten that, following the international reparations conference in June 1922 that levels of inflation in Germany altered overnight to hyperinflation on an almost Zimbabwean scale, with the mark slipping to 8000 marks per U.S. dollar by December. Simultaneously, as might have been expected, the cost of living soared by 16 times, creating the perfect breeding-ground for mothers with postnatal depression.

It is instructive to compare Germany's fascist experience with that of Norway, one of the first countries to be occupied by Nazi Germany (April 9, 1940) and the very last that the Nazis relinquished (May 8, 1945: weeks after Adolf Hitler was dead in his bunker.)

Vidkun Quisling created a Norwegian fascist party called National Gathering, which enjoyed close links with Nazi Germany, but which never managed to win more than 2.5% of Norwegian votes. Still, most Scandinavian countries had at least some level of support for Nazi Germany: Finland even joined Germany in the war against Soviet Union while Sweden, although technically neutral, still had many Nazi sympathizers (10,000 Swedish volunteers joined the Finns against Stalin.)

It remains instructive to compare pro-Nazi sympathies in Germany and Norway. Germany lost millions (soldiers and civilians) during WWI, while hyperinflation, 40% unemployment and the stock market crash of 1929 meant that millions of women and mothers faced misery along with financial hardship and that postnatal depression was more or less the norm. Most (though certainly not all) Nazi sympathizers were young men and women and it's not hard to imagine—especially if one happened to be a youthful narcissist—the attraction of rampaging around German towns taking out one's frustrations by beating up communists, socialists and Jews—or indeed anybody failing to do the Nazi salute with sufficient enthusiasm.

However in Norway, Vidkun Quisling's National Gathering, despite a message strikingly similar to that of the German Nazis, made little headway in popular support. First of all Norway had been neutral during WWI, so no Norwegian soldiers died. Secondly Norway had never endured hyperinflation like Germany's (indeed, no country did). In fact, Norway is on the whole a wealthy country with strong shipping, fishing, agricultural and manufacturing industries, so Norwegian mothers might be expected to have suffered much less postnatal depression and consequently raised fewer narcissists than their German counterparts. This doesn't mean that there were no narcissists in Norway, only that the soil for raising them was less fertile. Norway simply lacked the enough appetite for fascism—and consequently suffered considerably during the Nazi occupation.

I believe that this is a theory never before advanced about Vidkun Quisling and his party, in relation to the Nazis. I firmly believe that historians have completely missed the main reason so many (and so quickly) leapt to support the Nazis in Germany. Deep down I can't believe that German people are in any way different from any other people: they simply had—through a combination of circumstances—at that time a far higher proportion of narcissists than any other European country. Adolf Hitler and his message of hatred had far more chance of attracting votes in Germany than in anywhere else.

It's important to realise that nobody wants to be known as a narcissist. Most people on the narcissistic spectrum make great efforts to be looked upon as caring, whether it is by gently holding little babies or patting his dog for the camera (both ruses employed by Hitler). Anything to look as normal and natural as possible while in the privacy of one's home relishing the German public's reactions as the Reichstag burns, or the misery of captured Russian forces, or the terror the Jews suffered when crammed into inhumane transport trains or even when gassed.

Normal people find this almost impossible to comprehend, but what I can't understand is that mothers all around the world, including those living in the very wealthiest countries, still today endure undiagnosed postnatal depression and consequently bring up children with the potential to become malignant narcissists. We cling to lost ideals, because we long to believe that damaged people can be cured. The truth (that narcissistics on the level about which I write cannot be helped, by drugs or by psychiatry) is just too much for most people to bear. There is a huge unwillingness to believe, because until we have accepted the crucial connection between postnatal depression and malignant narcissism not much will change.

The fact is, we are all born with the potential for good, but severely depressed mothers can unwittingly twist us into malignant narcissists. The reason why this happens is very hard for most people to accept because the time-lapse between mothering a baby and recognising the crime of a grown-up malignant narcissist might be anywhere between fifteen and even forty years—while the last thing a criminologist is likely to investigate is the narcissist's experience in his first three years.

But to return to Germany and Norway between the wars, Norway's situation was very different. First of all, it remained neutral during WWI, so it didn't lose vast numbers of young men. Secondly, Norway was (and is) on the whole a wealthy country with shipping, fishing, agriculture and manufacturing—certainly without rampant inflation—so the mothers of its youth would have suffered much less. Many fewer mothers in Norway than in Germany suffered post-natal depression, and however hard he tried, Quisling couldn't get most Norwegians interested in his own fascist party.

Thus levels of postnatal depression—and eventually, National Socialism and radicalism in general—were fed by economic despair. I'm not saying that every single youth who joined Hitler Youth, the SA, or the SS etc. were necessarily children of mothers with postnatal depression: that would be absurd. But what I do suspect is that it was a factor largely ignored until now in the attraction of a party with such inherently sadistic values.

Yet the General Theory of Postnatal Depression and Malignant Narcissism does not only attempt to explain Adolf Hitler as a narcissistic phenomenon, it also suggests why so many Germans espoused the Nazis as a party. And the theory does not end there: it is applicable to both historical and sociological phenomena.

Now we'll consider another example: Saddam Hussein.

Saddam Hussein

Few characters cry out to be included in this book as powerfully as Saddam Hussein. As already mentioned, his father deserted his mother six months before Saddam was born, while his 13-year-old brother died of cancer shortly after the birth.

A huge amount of research has been done into Saddam Hussein: how he was known as the "Butcher of Baghdad" as a young man—not to mention how he worked as a contract killer against any "enemy" of the Ba'ath Party, pushing and shoving until he made it to the top by finding conspiracies around every corner (and inventing them when necessary—a method used by most narcissists, whether in City offices, Stalin's Soviet Union or Mao's China).

Although Ahmed Hassan was called President from 1969–1979, in reality Saddam Hussein possessed the real power, including involving himself in many plots and assassinations—as well as adroitly positioning himself to take over. When Ahmed Hassan finally died in 1979 Saddam simply did what he had already primed himself to do.

In common with Hitler, Stalin and Mao, Hussein led Iraq on a circuitously bloody path of wars, misery and political witch-hunts. Here are a few statistics:

1) Saddam Hussein attempted his first assassination when he was only fourteen.
2) The Iran-Iraq war lasted from 1980 to 1988, leaving half a million Iraqi dead along with 1 million Iranians.

3) The Iraqi invasion of Kuwait in 1990 was followed by the invasion under UN auspices into both Kuwait and Iraq.
4) 9/11 led to the invasion and overthrowing of Saddam Hussein, and to his execution by hanging.

Saddam Hussein was a grandiose style of narcissist, someone who rose to power by inventing conspiracies wherever possible and who relished the anguish of others. This is most obviously apparent during the (videotaped) event of August 1, 1979, during a party assembly—a bizarre and terrifying occasion. Guards suddenly stalked in, the doors were locked, and in front of petrified party members, sixty-eight names of "traitors" were inexorably read out, while—one by one—party members were hauled forth before their colleague and marched out towards a destiny of torture, execution and/or prison.

The video (available on YouTube, if one has the stomach for it) gives a strong sense of the sheer terror in the room while the names are called out. Fascinatingly, meanwhile, Saddam Hussein calmly smoked his cigar, while enjoying every second of he event: the sweating faces of the delegates in the hall, the shock of the denounced, the almost palpable fear. It's as if he could taste it as well as his own cigar, and he loved the taste. There is no doubt in my mind that this is the true Saddam Hussein—or that he watched the video of that event over and over again. (Similarly Saddam's gassing of an estimated 200,000 Kurds—which occurred between 1986 to 1989—must have given him vicious satisfaction.)

In short, Saddam Hussein's appetite for terror knew no limits. Like Hitler he basically lost touch with reality, creating a huge number of enemies inside his country (not to mention the rest of the world) that would eventually lead to his own downfall.

Again like Hitler the driving force in Saddam was to thrill to the maximum fear and despair in other's faces. After some of his political witch-hunts he carried such behaviour to the ultimate extent, even arranging for for relatives to execute their own relatives to prove their loyalty to him. (What better way for a narcissist to double or treble the amount of despair? One can only imagine Saddam's savage thrill when a father was forced to shoot his son or a son his father! No wonder that someone so sick imagined and invented conspiracies at will—or that his true idol was Stalin himself.)

"The law is anything that I write on a piece of paper," Saddam Hussein once bragged, and, along with many dictators he also claimed that "God has selected my life for me!" "I know a traitor before he knows himself!" he also opined, while simultaneously inventing a traitorous plot that just happened to involve several people who had showed the slightest hesitation in supporting him 100%. (Ironically, Saddam Hussein loved to make films portraying himself as a hero of the people.)

Of course, like Hitler, he was fooling nobody. Saddam Hussein will go down in history as one of the most blood-thirsty dictators in history after Hitler, Stalin and Mao and—just like them—the key to understanding his condition was during his first three years of life when his mother almost certainly endured a deep-seated postnatal depression and entirely failed to relate to him emotionally.

Of course, not all narcissists operate on so vast a scale.

Internet Stalking And Narcissistic Behavior

Why is internet stalking and school bullying on the rise in developed countries? Don't we live in a world with more knowledge, greater wealth, and more state-aided welfare than ever before?

Yes—at least in the West. The trouble is that the internet is first and foremost a tool: and that like any tool it can be used for purposes both good and evil.

Take, for example, Ruth Jeffery, whose case hit the headlines in February 2012, because she had been cyber-stalked by her own boyfriend, Shane Webber.

It started as a normal romance. They were young, fell in love, and when they moved to different places, still remained in daily contact, through email, Skype and Facebook. Eventually they moved in together and Ruth started University. However, one day Shane burst into the bathroom (while Ruth was washing) and started to take naked photos of her. Later, naked photos of Ruth started to appear on Internet porn sites.

Shane claimed that his computer had been hacked, but this happened again, until eventually the photos started to appear mentioning Ruth's real name. Unsurprisingly, Ruth became traumatized, and also developed Obsessive Compulsive Disorder. She started locking the front door to her apartment more than thirteen times every time that she left because she felt so nervous that somebody might stage a break-in, and to switch all the lights off at least thirteen times in order to feel confident that they really were switched off. She became increasingly depressed and her friends started to get strange emails from her in which she accused them of being involved in the stalking. She also (unsurprisingly) became more and more isolated, turning more and more to her boyfriend, Shane, for comfort.

Once, her parents dared to suggest that it could have been Shane behind all the internet photos but Ruth denied it hotly—mostly because Shane had sworn that he had not done anything—instead he had framed his own friend Lee Evans, who had access to both the computers. Ruth believed Shane and complained to the police, who warned Lee Evans to keep away from Ruth. Shane even wrote an angry letter to Lee, passionately blaming him for exploiting photos of Shane's girlfriend . . . Meanwhile still more photos appeared on various porn sites, some with Ruth's name—and a few even with her phone number. Men called Ruth around the clock, until she became too nervous even to dare to leave the house.

This went on for years, and probably could have gone on indefinitely, had not Ruth's father received an email from someone pretending to be Ruth. The email was addressed to "Daddy" but Ruth had never called him by that name, and the email even included three nude photos of Ruth. Ruth's father managed to trace the email to its source, and learned that it was Shane Webber. (Powerfully relieved, he even cried out, "Gotcha!") It was as he had long suspected: his daughter was being stalked by her own boyfriend.

There are estimated to be approximately 2.5 million stalkers in Great Britain: roughly 4% of the population (with similar figures in the USA). Most stalkers are never reported: like school bullying it remains hidden, being considered shameful, either to the institution or to the person concerned.

Cases as extreme as Ruth's come to light for one reason only: because Shane was convicted, receiving four months in prison and an injunction never again to contact Ruth. Her mental health had suffered terribly, yet had it not been for her father's computer expertise it could have ended even more tragically. (It's not uncommon in such cases for paranoia or even psychosis to develop, and for suicides to occur.)

R. D. Lang, the distinguished psychiatrist, claimed that, when practicing on depressed or on schizophrenic patients (given time and therapy) he could cure anybody, but that after the patient had returned home, after some months or perhaps a year they were likely to be back in therapy again, having been made ill again. Lang therefore concluded that the problem was in the home environment rather than with the patients themselves.

Similarly, Swedish psychologist Elgar Jonsson wrote a book called <u>Tokfurstena</u> (roughly translated: <u>The Emperor of Fools</u>). The most remarkable thing about Jonsson was that he himself endured schizophrenia, and, had not a female psychiatrist taken him under her wing, he might to this day be incarcerated in a Swedish mental institution. When asked what schizophrenia was he considered and finally said: "It's a strategy that people choose when they can't cope with reality. Some people have done me so much harm that I can't see them anymore."

To return to Ruth: her boyfriend Shane had systematically worked on her, slowly and steadily pushing her into both depression and OCD (in fact, had she not had supportive parents she might well have developed a still more debilitating condition). Despite this, Ruth eventually became so ill that Shane was obliged to drive her to appointments, make sure she took her medications, while—and this is a crucial point—Shane was being lauded for his kindness and support. Far from being an unlikely scenario, the question is whether it isn't far more common than generally perceived. Even after Shane's trial, Ruth loyally attempted to explain it all by stating that Shane was jealous and possessive, which led him to treat her so horrifically.

And yet I believe that Ruth's experience is not particularly exceptional. According to Professor Robert Hare, Shane is simply a perfect example of a malignant narcissist: or, in other words, someone whose main life-efforts are bent towards figuring out how to create despair in others. (With regard to Ruth, of course, Shane succeeded brilliantly. Having said which, he was uninterested in conning Ruth out of money so he fails to qualify as a sociopath.)

The main question still persists. Why are normal, intelligent citizens conned by such people?

To put it another way: Ruth might just as easily have been a victim of school bullying for many years, suffered quietly and perhaps one day committed suicide. She would then have been reckoned just one more teenage suicide tragedy. Alternatively she might have been bullied at work, until one day she resigned (or else was fired, having served his sadistic purpose, probably by the very person who had bullied her). But neither of these things occurred.

The fascinating thing about this case is that it highlights beautifully how Shane operated (quietly, in the background) while still spreading rumours among Ruth's friends that she no longer cared to see them anymore—although in fact the exact opposite was the case. It's not hard to see how malignant narcissists like Shane operate, even systematically pretending to love their partner, and yet thrilling to their misery. So the question arises: why did he do it? Didn't he constantly reassure Ruth that he loved her? Didn't he swear—over and over—that he was innocent?

Of course he did. But the fundamental truth about narcissists involves two terrible truths: an utter lack of remorse and a terrifying inability to feel love. In short, for Shane to say, "I love you, Ruth," meant exactly nothing, as we've already seen. (After all, why would he repeatedly post naked pictures of someone he "loved" on porn sites? It wasn't for his own gratification: He could see her naked whenever he wanted to.)

I have no intention of writing the kind of book that will waffle vaguely around the surface of the issues. Instead, my plan is to grab the narcissist "by the balls", explaining who he is and (most of all) how he became whom he became—because, sadly, there are millions of Shanes out there, of whom only a tiny fraction get dragged into court and an even smaller fraction end up in prison.

It was Shane's arrogance that made him vulnerable. Had Shane never dared to write to Ruth's father, Ruth might to this day have continued to believe that she had attracted some mystery stalker, or that the whole world hated her, or—still worse—that she was nothing more than any other "normal" woman whose nudity could be exploited on porn sites.

From her father's courage and determination, however, she eventually learned the truth. And, as is surely obvious, what Shane did to Ruth is absolutely classic narcissistic behaviour. Little by little he tested the water: planting naked pictures of Ruth and watching how she gradually and tearfully deteriorated while still passionately referring to her tormenter as her "dearest friend and best support."

In short, we need to accept that narcissists are not like us. The narcissist is unburdened by compassion: instead he has an agenda that I hope (in later chapters) to explain and explore. Meanwhile it needs to be made clear to the reader that the narcissist follows the same pattern he has followed since childhood and that (like Shane), he is every bit as addicted to conjuring up expressions of despair as a drug addict is addicted to his drug. In fact the narcissist has a still stronger addiction because, as Professor Hare notes, there is no cure. (Interestingly, Professor Hare also suggests that it is common practice for the imprisoned narcissist to use and manipulate the prison psychologist, perhaps to suddenly be diagnosed as schizophrenic in order to be moved to a more agreeable venue such as a mental hospital—and later, when bored by the mental institution, to suddenly "recover" from schizophrenia in hopes of being shoved back to prison again (or even to "become" a Christian, convincing the prison pastor, in order to gain a recommendation for early release.)

So: Why did Shane behave as he did? This is not a book about Shane, but Shane matters here, because Shane is merely a perfect example of how narcissists can operate, manipulating all Ruth's friends and family, blaming his own "best friends", but most of all owning the constant narcissistic pleasure in observing Ruth getting deeper and deeper in despair, day after day.

The ultimate goal of the narcissist, sociopath or psychopath is to break down the victim (their prey) into utter despair. Their methods might be different but the end result is always the same, whether it's Bernhard Madhoff's victims losing their life savings and sometimes committing suicide or Ruth steadily deteriorating emotionally and psychologically. (Indeed, had Ruth not had a suspicious father than it is possible that Ruth could have developed a full-blown psychosis—and who could possibly have blamed her?)

In short, the ultimate goal for the narcissist is to break the victim, completely and thoroughly. In Shane's case, we can observe that he constantly increased the pressure on Ruth by sending more and more naked photos to various porn sites, propelling her deeper and deeper into despair. (We can also see how Shane might have had no difficulty in lying to Ruth that it was not he but others who had betrayed her. Shane was prepared to do anything and say anything in order to continue the narcissistic game.) In fact, for Shane and for malignant narcissists in general, their victims' despair is itself priceless. Oddly enough, psychiatry, criminology, sociology, economics, business and history alike remain silent on this subject, nor is it widely recognized that around 10% of the population are narcissistic, whether in the form of pure narcissism or (the still closely-related) sociopathy and psychopathy (see Prof. Robert Hare).

If Ruth hadn't had a father who decided to become an internet detective, tracing the emails to their origin, then her story could very well have had a more terrible outcome. Ruth might today be one of thousands of patients in some mental institution, perhaps suffering from paranoia, depression or even schizophrenia. Shane, judging from his previous form, would doubtless come on regular visits, not only providing tragic evidence of the latest porn sites where her photos had appeared, but and at the same time bringing chocolate and sympathy while typifying the "caring, concerned" boyfriend.

In this case, not to mention a huge number of similar cases in both the UK and the USA, it's the narcissists who deliberately run a private campaign hoping to make people mentally ill and/or to cause them to break down into despair. (The more despair the more narcissistic joy.)

Here we have a case clearly showing how a narcissist can, without compunction, make his girlfriend mentally ill. He knew exactly how to break her, how to deceive her and how to manipulate her friends and relatives. Worse still, I have no doubt that when Shane comes out from prison, smarter and still more expert at manipulation after psychotherapy, he will almost certainly find a new victim or victims.

I have been asked whether psychotherapy might be able to cure narcissists like Shane. Instead it will almost certainly only make people like Shane slicker and smarter and better able to choose a still more vulnerable victim the next time around. There is no cure for narcissism: instead this is how Shane's brain developed during his first three years of life. No psychotherapy in the world or medication can change that.

How many people subsist in mental institutions today because they happen to have been unlucky enough to have some like Shane in their emotional lives, whether as boyfriend, husband, father, mother, friend or other relative? I doubt whether anyone has bothered to research this question: plus, it is clearly no part of any psychiatrist's agenda to find out, especially considering that sedation in mental institutions is used to keep many "mentally ill" patients nicely manageable for ever.

Would staff in such a mental institution ever have figured out that Shane was behind it all? I doubt it, mostly because Ruth herself failed to realise and, when challenged, even defended Shane. So we have to ask the question: how many people are in mental institutions today because of narcissistics like Shane?

The answer is that we simply don't know for sure, but it must happen. In the first place, psychiatrists can simply get it wrong. Secondly, many psychiatrists are themselves narcissistic, and would feel an enormous narcissistic "buzz" in having someone like Ruth as a patient. It isn't impossible that they might even enjoy discussing all her naked pictures on porn sites, conceivably sending Ruth even deeper into madness and paranoia, while writing coolly in some medical journal that "Ruth had a severe if latent mental disorder that only fully manifested itself in therapy".

Later I hope to elucidate how a narcissist like Shane became the kind of person he eventually became. With this in mind I will next consider an even more terrifying malignant narcissist than Shane.

Daniel Lynch Accid Attack Of Katie Piper

In 2008, when Katie Piper replied to a flirtatious Facebook message from Daniel Lynch, she had no notion that he was a narcissist who had already served almost five years in prison for throwing boiling water in the face of another man. Lynch instead presented himself as a successful property developer and martial arts expert who had studied computing at a University in London and who only lived with his mother because it was convenient to his martial art gym.

In fact, these were almost all lies. Instead Daniel Lynch had picked out Katie Piper partly because she was exceptionally beautiful but most of all because she was also kind, generous, naïve and thus, from a narcissistic point of view, perfect narcissistic prey.

Katie Piper worked as a model, and occasionally as a TV presenter. Although she had only worked as an extra in TV series (including <u>Eastenders</u> and <u>The Bill)</u> her acting career was certainly on the rise.

After less than two weeks, during which the couple had gone out to various events and restaurants, there were a couple of warning signs that Katie chose to ignore. For example, Daniel had been furious when Katie took him into a gay bar. Astonished, she advised him to relax and that the gay guys would leave him alone, which they did. On another occasion a shopkeeper innocently said, "Here you are, love," to Katie. Daniel was deeply affronted, and Katie had to quieten him by observing that the shopkeeper didn't mean anything by it. On several other occasions Daniel became angry about similar events, which seemed to Katie utterly trivial.

Katie's nightmare really started when Daniel suggested that they should spend the night in a hotel. This certainly didn't turn out the way she'd hoped. A normal man would have been gentle and romantic, and tried to seduce Katie with warmth and irresistible passion. But Daniel is a narcissist: it's impossible for him to have an emotional relationship with anybody and once he got Katie into the hotel room he proceeded to do what he had presumably planned all along: to rape her and to revel in her despair.

Worse still, when Katie tried to flee he pushed her head into a glass wall in the hotel room, and as her head started to bleed he raped her again. After some time he brought her into the bathroom and, coolly taking out a razor blade, he started talking about cutting up her face. Katie, of course, was utterly bewildered, but for Daniel and other malignant narcissists, such a threat made perfect sense, since it was bound to accelerate Katie's despair, while to Daniel Katie was by then nothing more than narcissistic prey: prey that he intended to feed off for as long as possible.

Next he took his belt from his trousers, attached the belt to the bathroom door and advised Katie to avoid more pain and humiliation by hanging herself on the belt. Katie, petrified, pleaded for her life.

After many hours of other horrific events, the pair eventually left the hotel together, and after repeatedly promising Daniel that she loved him "far too much" to report him to the police, Katie finally reached the safety of her own apartment. There she confessed to her flat-mates all that had happened. Naturally, they urged her to get in contact with the police but Katie refused (she was afraid of Daniel and believed that he could revenge himself on her, whatever she did).

After a couple of days and many telephone calls, Daniel phoned Katie and told her to go to a local internet cafe to read his email. Daniel was speaking on the phone with Katie as she left her apartment and walked down the street. As they talked, a strange-looking young man approached the girl from across the street holding a paper cup between his hands. Assuming he was begging, Katie reached for her purse, while he threw the contents of the cup—acid—into her face. Acid scorched her face and eyes, ran down her neck and between her breasts, raking her skin with indescribable pain. Poor Katie let out a scream like a tortured animal—while Daniel, who had organised and arranged the attack, remained on the phone, probably relishing every sound. (Indeed he probably recorded the conversation so that her reaction could be played back over and over again.)

This appalling story elucidates the core of narcissism, which most people just can't comprehend, beyond words like "sick, monster, psychopath." Daniel Lynch is a malignant narcissist and this is what narcissistic people do. They are simply addicted to the kind of behaviour that creates maximum anguish in the victim. It's even possible that he planned this long before he selected Katie Piper as prey. What he saw in Katie was a particularly beautiful woman, whose career partly depended on her looks. He probably reasoned that her despair would that much the greater upon losing her beauty, because she had more beauty to lose.

I find it strange how—in 2013—psychiatrists fail to understand that he is as he always will be, and that no psychotherapy in the world can cure him. (In prison he even apparently "groomed" a female prison guard for his own purposes, but the seduction attempt was uncovered.)

Only a fool could believe that putting Daniel Lynch in jail will make it less likely that future mothers with postnatal depression will raise future narcissists. When it comes to crime, decade after decade we fish for solutions in the wrong waters.

But it's time to move on.

Ted Bundy, Serial Killer

It's hard to imagine a more intelligent, charismatic or handsome young fellow than Ted Bundy, a law and psychology student with a taste for criminology and and good-looking young women. The slim, fit, American cheerleader sort was Ted Bundy's "type" and he was born to be any mother-in-law's dream: polite, articulate and humorous, he was adept at making people believe that he would be a great "catch".

Ted Bundy was convicted of 35 murders but the true number is believed to be far higher, perhaps even a hundred higher. All of his victims were young women who in many cases offered to assist him when he appeared with his arm or leg in plaster. It's hard to imagine a good-natured girl refusing to help a wounded young man carry a surfing board to his Volkswagen. This was the car where had removed the front passage seat so he could with greater ease tie up his victim, rape her and (it is believed, though not proven) strangle her during the sex act. For someone like Bundy, the victim's despair combined with a slow strangulation during the rape would be the ultimate narcissistic "high".

Ted Bundy was arrested several times without being charged, but during his last free period he visited Florida State University. Over several terrifying days he broke into various places on campus. In some cases he beat women to death without raping them, and in other cases he used a piece of wood to render them unconscious so that they would be able to recall absolutely nothing. While they were "out" he bit sections of their bodies as a revolting memento. No doubt it gave Ted Bundy enormous narcissistic joy to know that those of his victims whose lives he had chosen to spare would still awaken in horror to find teeth-marks on their bodies. (Fortunately, Florida was a last desperate narcissistic joyride before Bundy was finally arrested, put on trial and eventually executed.)

This is not a book about Bundy, but a book about how mothers with postnatal depression can't relate to their babies during the first few years. Ted Bundy fits this profile perfectly. His mother, Eleanor Cowell, later Eleanor Bundy, told her family that she became pregnant by a passing sailor. Unluckily, hers was a highly religious family headed by a hugely dominant father who no doubt hurled a lot of mental abuse on her. (It is even conjectured that there was no "sailor" and that Eleanor had been raped by her own father.) In either case, he certainly forced her to bring up her son Ted more as a sibling than as a son: Bundy was apparently not even told who his real mother was. It's not hard to see how enormous family pressure plus culturally unacceptable childbirth could have thrown Eleanor into deep postnatal depression.

A Freudian might very well try and portray Bundy as having a latent hatred against women because his mother and grandparents refused to admit who his mother was. I doubt this, however, simply because Ted Bundy just did what all malignant narcissists do, only rather more spectacularly than most: enjoy creating despair for others. (A pastor tried to get Ted Bundy to agree that pornography had led him astray,but amongst Ted's belongings the only pornography discovered was a men's magazine called Cheerleaders.)

However, there is a tale about the three-year-old Ted Bundy. Early one morning he collected all the kitchen knives and spread them out on his visiting aunt's bed. Then he stood gleefully waiting until she awoke, astonished and terrified, to find all the knives surrounding her on the bed and little Ted glowing with narcissistic delight. By the age of three, Ted Bundy could have been a skilled narcissist who could scheme, plan and carefully choose his victims.

But we'll now consider someone who couldn't stop killing people: the so-called "Doctor of death".

Doctor Of Death

DOCTOR OF DEATH
Nobody that we know about was better at fooling the public better than Dr Harold Shipman in Hyde, United Kingdom.

A bearded, paternal-looking family doctor, or so it seemed, emerged from his middle-class home when rumors first started to circulate that perhaps not everything was quite right in Hyde, a small town in middle England. Dr Shipman calmly walked up to the TV camera, tilted his head confidingly and in a calm, reassuring voice informed us that his patient concerned had, "died of old age". Clearly, there was nothing to worry about. Or was there?

There were certainly rumours. There was a taxi-driver who—too frequently for coincidence, in his opinion—drove old ladies to Dr Shipman's surgery only to find out that they had, one after another, died. After he recorded over twenty instances the taxi-driver went to the police. Unluckily though the police worked very slowly, probably because it was hard for them to believe what had been suggested. (To be fair, probably most police forces wouldn't have given immediate credence to such a story.)

Then an alert female doctor noticed that the mortality rate in Hyde was higher than one might have expected, and started to worry about harmful minerals in the water supply.

However, what finally gave the game away was Shipman's greed. With his last victim Dr Shipman decided to fake a false will, supposedly leaving the old lady's house to him. Unfortunately for Shipman (but hugely fortunately for everyone else) the lady's daughter was a lawyer. She took Shipman to court for falsifying a will and while they were checking him out the police thought they might as well take another glance at a few of his patients' deaths. The breakthrough came when they checked his personal computer, and noticed an instance when Shipman had entered a comment about his patient's death <u>before</u> she had actually died. Dr Shipman was eventually put to trial and found guilty of killing twenty older ladies. But this turned out to be only a modest proportion of his murders.

Dr Shipman is believed to have certainly killed around 200 older women and there are unresolved suspicions involving around another 200, Dr Shipman might well have killed over 400 people —and some people consider the true figure might be as high as 500. (He makes Hollywood's Hannibal Lecter resemble somebody's friendly uncle, in comparative terms.)

My understanding is that Dr Shipman killed some of his victims in the patients' own homes and some in his surgery (as the taxi driver observed). Most occurred thanks to an overdose of morphine. However, the interesting bit is that at some point after the death Dr Shipman would phone a relative, often the patient's adult daughter. These conversations apparently followed a pattern something like this:

"This is Dr Shipman. It's regarding your mother."

"What's the problem? Is she all right?"

"Well you know that she's an old frail woman."

"Yes, of course."

"And that she's not been very well for a long time."

"You mean she's ill?"

"I think you start to understand."

"You mean, she is—"

"Yes."

"She's actually—"

"I think you start to understand."

"She's <u>dead</u>?"

"Now you start to understand."

In short, Dr Shipman got part of his narcissistic "kicks" from stringing along his patient's daughter or other close relative. Did he record the conversations? I suspect he did, so that he could listen to the conversations over and over again, possibly while masturbating. Unlike Adolf Hitler we're not talking here about pure narcissism. As far as we know Hitler's narcissism did not coalesce with his sexual interests. But I wouldn't be surprised if it turned out that Dr Shipman masturbated while listening to the tapes with the appalled relatives, especially when the people he was deceiving were younger women. What a narcissistic treat! (Was it even possible that Dr Shipman chose certain old ladies because they had young or attractive daughters who might break down if told about her mother's unexpected death?)

Imagine what might have happened had Dr Shipman had actually moved home every now and then, instead of living in Hyde for 26 years—or if he had emigrated, say, to Australia or the USA. Had he kept moving, taxi drivers and fellow doctors would have been much less likely to become suspicious. Morphine would still have been available, as would his "kicks". We would never ever have heard of him and he could still be active "helping" older ladies to this day. It's even possible that there are other, less complacent Shipmans still out there, doing exactly that: killing and gloating—but moving on.

The Norway Shootings

I had already written most of this book when I heard that first a bomb had exploded in central Oslo and then that a single gunman had gone to Utøya, in Tyrifjorden, Buskerud and shot a great number of young people at point-blank range. Possibly uniquely, I had only one question: "Did Anders Behring Breivik's mother, Wenche Behring, suffer postnatal depression when he was born, or not?" (You can probably guess the answer.)

Wenche Behring was a divorced nurse with three children when she first moved to London and there met and married Jens David Breivik, an economist working the Norwegian Embassy. They had one child together, Anders Behring Breivik—and then, when the baby was still only aged one, they were divorced. Jens had met his new wife, Tove Øvermo, while working at the Embassy. We can only speculate as to when the pair started to get intimate, but a good guess might be when Wenche was pregnant with Anders.

At any rate at some point, whether while still pregnant or when looking after a (very) young baby, Wenche learned that her husband was unfaithful and her marriage was over. Alone in a strange country, with three other children from her first marriage and with very little support, we can only imagine Wenche's despair. There's no doubt that she became deeply depressed (whether or not she had actual postnatal depression). It is thus hugely unlikely that she could relate emotionally to baby Anders during the first three years of his life.

The mass killings remain hard for Norwegians to understand. After all, from their perspective: Breivik came from a good family, had no criminal convictions and nobody in his family had ever had any problems with the law. They wonder: Is he part of a right-wing movement (as he claims) or is he clinically insane? There is a country-wide hope, I believe, that he's "mad," so that everyone can simply say, "He's a lunatic, but now everything's OK again."

It has been reported that Breivik has shown absolutely no remorse, and firmly believes to this day that he was "saving" Europe from "a Muslim invasion" by killing junior members of the Norwegian Socialist party. (Sounds rather like Adolf Hitler, doesn't it?)—and this is my point, because Breivik and Hitler had one critical thing in common: mothers that endured postnatal depression. In every other respect: country, cultural background, lifestyle, they differ.

According to the press, Anders Behring Breivik spent nine years planning it all. It's easy to imagine the excitement he must have felt when his Oslo bomb detonated—not to mention his powerful joy as he targeted the teenagers, feeding off the panic and shock in their expressions and their (usually doomed) attempts to escape. I have no doubt that he relives the horrors of that day with deep contentment.

It's unsurprisingly difficult for a malignant narcissist to murder people and still be regarded as normal, which is where Breivik's crazy political manifesto comes in. Apparently it consists of over 1500 pages, espousing ultra-nationalism, Islamophobia, Zionism, anti-feminism and white Nationalism. Does this remind anyone else of Mein Kampf?

In short, had Breivik simply gone out and killed a lot of people because he liked the feeling of power, everyone would definitely have regarded him as a madman. So instead he invented what he (at least) fancied as a justification for his evil, presenting himself as a political knight in shining armour rather than what he is: a hopeless malignant narcissist, capable of feeling neither compassion nor remorse. Those brain connections were never formed during his first few years, and it's all far too late for him now. (He has even "apologised"—not for his crimes, but for not killing more people!)

In Norway, unsurprisingly, they have no notion what to do with him. First they declared him insane. Then they reversed their decision, put him on trial and convicted him. Since a life sentence in Norway is normally merely a maximum of 22 years they have had to pass a special law, in order to keep Breivik locked up for ever.

Experts suggest that approximately 75% of narcissists are men. The reason for this could be higher level of testosterone, but I believe it possible that woman relate more naturally and easily to baby girls. (Apparently Breivik's mother was a feminist and this could have contributed towards her feelings—or lack of them—towards her son.)

Feminism is widespread in all Scandinavian countries, especially in that most liberal variety, who view absolute equality as the goal (that women should amount to 50% in terms of government, corporations, professional occupations etc.). However, there are also those truly furious feminists, who view men—all men—as nothing more than animals with dildos between their legs. It is not hard to see how such militant feminists can be categorized as narcissistic, especially as in Scandinavia it is often the norm for professional women to hand over their newborn after a few weeks or months to a nanny, nursery or childcare centre.

Professor Harald Ofstad, the Norwegian philosopher, wrote in his seminal work <u>Our Contempt for Weakness</u> how each of us carries deeply inside the tendency to despise weakness. It was written during the post-Nazi occupation of Norway, in which Ofstad explained that each of us is capable of evil acts, just like the Nazis. Of course Ofstad never understood about the narcissistic spectrum—or that the usual moral laws and customs simply don't apply, to them at least.

In modern Norway, in common with all Scandinavian countries, it would be regarded as impossibly politically incorrect to opine that postnatal depression in the mother (and/or childcare before the age of three) might be the main reason why Breivik became the monster he turned into. The problem in practically all Scandinavia is that, given the choice between the crucial welfare of babies before the age of three and career opportunities for mothers, the babies are usually the ones to suffer.

This is why (I grieve to say) the Norway shootings might not be the last. Breivik might have had a mother demolished by postnatal depression, but the next killer might very well have had too many early years dealt with by uncaring nannies in some overcrowded nursery.

In Norway, liberal homeland of the Nobel Peace Prize, it is of course a huge embarrassment to have a home-grown serial killer: and when the psychiatrists came to the conclusion that he was "schizophrenic" the government doubtless felt a huge relief that they wouldn't have to stage a public trial, with all the international attention that it would bring. And yet, as we all know by now, it wouldn't take much from a smart and educated killer to act schizophrenic —nor would it be either the first or the last time in history that a serial killer fooled a psychiatrist.

Apparently the idea of the murders had obsessed Breivik for over nine years. His problem was obvious: when you detonate a huge car bomb (even one outside the house of the prime minister) you can never guarantee who might happen to be passing at the time, including children as in his own case (similarly, during 9/11 a striking number of those murdered in New York were foreigners, whether tourists or immigrants—not the people Al-Qaeda had in mind).

It has to be said that the narcissist lives in his own fantasy world, so <u>in Breivik's mind</u> it was primarily members of the Norwegian socialist party who were blown to pieces. He must have fantasised about the impact of the bomb many times and when it comes to the shooting at point-blank range he must have been in narcissistic heaven: to have such utter control over others—and to be so powerful in maximizing misery!

In this respect Breivik is in no way unusual amongst narcissists. Ted Bundy strangled his victims while watching their faces and possibly even sustaining an orgasm. Adolf Hitler ordered his enemies' executions filmed so that he could gloat over their agonies again and again. Sutcliffe became sexually aroused through killing women. We can safely presume that Breivik will even now be thumbing through all his shootings in his mind, over and over again: surely enough horrific memories even for a lifetime in jail.

It's hard, perhaps even almost impossible, for normal peopleto accept that the narcissist, sociopath and psychopath are simply "not like us"—and never can be. We almost long to believe that people like Breivik destroyed other's lives through political conviction: not because we have such faith in politics but because some (very human) part of us seeks in vain for some excuse. (Another part of us longs to believe that at the other extreme that they are simply insane.) It will probably be hard for most readers to accept that the way their brain cells are hardwired mean that they are addicted to the despair in other people's faces—and that any apparent extreme political convictions are probably merely a cover-up for the truth that they are <u>morally</u> insane.

Science, in common with subjects including philosophy, psychology, criminology, history, economics and business, has yet to come to terms with the fact that perhaps 10% of the population in countries like Great Britain and

How mothers with postnatal depression...

USA are either narcissists, sociopaths or psychopaths to some degree or other (In Scandinavian countries, because of near-compulsory childcare at a hugely young age, the percentage might very well be higher, although it is not politically correct to point this out.) This is a fact observed by British child psychologist Oliver James in his book How not to f**k them up and is an uncomfortable truth for Scandinavians to hear.

It might sound hopelessly Utopian for a career woman to take three years off to look after a child while expecting her job to be kept waiting for her. But there is no immediate shortage of children in the world and when a women loves her job more than her offspring than perhaps she should seriously consider instead procuring a hamster, goldfish, cat or dog, especially with the world's population is on its way to 10 billion.

There is not only no need for more babies generally but there is especially no need for more children who (because of parental neglect) develop into malignant narcissists, sociopaths and psychopaths. Militant feminists might choose to ignore the fact that ignored and neglected babies can become narcissists—or even welcome the fact in that such narcissists might well succeed in climbing to the top of the corporate ladder. (It is pointless to deny that narcissists in particular occupy top positions in large corporations, male narcissists particularly.) But this is the topic of my next book.

We need to move on.

The "Batman" Mass Shooting 2012

On 20 July 2012 James Holmes bought a ticket to the midnight showing in a cinema in Aurora, Colorado. Half an hour into the film he walked calmly to the emergency door and exited, first ensuring that the door couldn't lock shut behind him. He walked to his car, pulled on his bullet-proof clothing and armed himself with a shotgun, a semi-automatic rifle, a 40-caliber handgun, a gas-mask and two gas bombs.

Calmly he walked back to the cinema, tossed in the gas bombs and started to shoot through the fog. Starting with his 12-gauge shot-gun he later switched to his semi-automatic rifle. When this jammed he continued firing with his handgun. He started aiming at his victims from the back, but soon he stalked up and down the aisle, shooting to his left and right.

After the murders James Holmes surrendered to police, considerately telling them that he had also planted explosives in his apartment. (I wonder why he told them... perhaps to see their shocked reaction?)

He had murdered twelve people and, had not his magazine jammed after 40 rounds, the toll would have been far higher. James Holmes is an intelligent biology student who had been working towards a Ph.D., and he has since put a good deal of effort into persuading the world to believe that he became insane. But I believe that he is just a narcissist who knew exactly what he was doing, and that during the shooting he simply had a private narcissistic little party, calmly mowing down one terrified movie-goer after another while relishing his own sense of power and the helplessness and fear in their faces.

There are many similarities between Anders Breivik and James Holmes even although Breivik took the trouble to dress up his narcissistic deeds in twisted narcissistic logic over 1500 pages, while Holmes merely pretended insanity. (He also colored his hair red and told the police that he was "the Joker", a famous Batman villain, an excellent example of warped narcissistic humour. Just the sort that Hitler would have appreciated.)

We can only speculate whether James' mother (Arlen Holmes) endured postnatal depression, neglected James during his first three years of life or is herself a narcissist. His murders, I believe, can be firmly traced back to his first few years of life, where emotional interaction with his mother did not take place as it was meant to do. The very fact that he "fed off" the panic and terror suggests that he needed to provoke a violent reaction in others in order to feel "seen".

James Holmes' prosecutor, seeking the death penalty, claimed that James had told people four months prior to the shooting that he wanted to "kill people". Some Americans believe that the the existence of capital punishment can dissuade other violent men in the future: however, since the narcissistic brain is created before the age of three killing Holmes (or any other narcissistic murderer) will have absolutely no effect on the offspring of future damaged mothers who are utterly unable to relate to their babies. It might save the state of Colorado the trouble and expense of keeping Holmes in prison: that's the only good that might come of it.

Boston Marathon Bombing 2013

On 15 April 2013 the two brothers, Dzhokhar and Tamerlan Tsarnaev, each planted and detonated one bomb close to the finishing post of the Boston marathon, killing three bystanders and injuring 264. Rumours abound that Al Qaeda or other Islamic terrorist groups had encouraged them, but you won't be astonished to hear that my theory is different.

The brothers had been born Muslims in Tokamak, Uzbekistan, part of a deeply oppressed minority. Their home country had been invaded by the Nazis during the WWII, while the Soviet Union had not been notably kind to its citizens under Stalin. In addition, Muslims make up only 4% of the population in Uzbekistan. It's not difficult to understand why their parents decided to travel to the US on tourist visas and, once there, requested political asylum. Financial hardship, being part of an oppressed religious minority, near-constant fears of roving gangs and ethnic violence: all the ingredients were there necessary to push their mother Zubeidat into postnatal depression. (It must also be a very nervy step to leave one's country to beg for political asylum.) However, their mother would almost certainly have been deeply depressed before arriving in USA.

After the bombing it was postulated that the brothers had been brainwashed by Islamic extremists, because normal people don't commit acts of terrorism. (The surviving brother has encouraged this fantasy, as well as attempting to shift all the blame onto the elder brother.) The fact, of course, is that neither Dzhokhar or Tamerlan could ever have been completely normal, they are narcissists because their mother had severe postnatal depression.

"I don't have a single American friend. I don't understand them," Dzhokhar has been quoted as saying: but it is not that he dislikes Americans particularly, he can't relate emotionally to <u>anybody</u>. Like Ted Bundy people with this disorder can appear friendly and charming and give the impression of liking others, but deep down it's their sheer narcissistic joy to detonate bombs, while they thrill to cause mayhem and murder. The brothers probably fantasized about the Boston Marathon bombs for years, planning every detail (which is not to say that it would have been hard for them to have corresponded with some terrorist group: as joining Al Qaeda nowadays is only marginally harder than ordering an on-line pizza).

Then again, from Al Qaeda's point of view all they had to do is to give their blessing to the two brothers, telling them that "Good luck to you" and "Your place in heaven is secure". It wouldn't have cost them much, either in time or effort. The notion that the brothers would have to attend some Pakistani training camp is I believe grossly exaggerated because a narcissist is already self-trained, from an early age they have an innate longing to kill and destroy.

Believing that the Dzhokhar brothers are "normal" Muslim guys who were brainwashed by Al Qaeda sympathizers is not unlike believing that a friendly stork delivers babies. Narcissistic people do naturally, with a little bit of encouragement, what narcissistic people do. Like the "Yorkshire Ripper" pretending that God that ordered him to kill people because he was too embarrassed to admit his sick masturbation fantasy about battered women gasping for their last breath (for details, see Appendix 2).

Similarly Breivik dressed up his mass murders in some kind of politically queasy right-wing theory, to make it possible for him to relish his narcissistic bloodbath without believing himself to be evil.

Once the roots of narcissism become clear many jigsaw pieces fall into place. Closing down Al-Qaeda websites is probably a far better and cheaper option than bugging the whole world to find potential future terrorists. If the USA can spy on 6 billion people on the internet, than surely its government should be capable of closing down a few thousand Al-Qaeda websites? (Or perhaps the websites are too useful, as a means to identify potential terrorists?)

It's not hard to imagine an enormous building in Langley, Virginia, with thousands upon thousands of CIA employees monitoring calls through earphones and yet generally it's just some ordinary citizen who raises the alarm. British intelligence during the Cold War was flawed, to put it politely. There was a long list of MI5 and MI6 double agents in KGB employ, including Donald McLean, Guy Burgess, Kim Philby and Antony Blunt. It makes you wonder what use the secret services do, apart from running up huge tax bills, when in the end it is far more likely that an ordinary policeman will stop somebody for a trivial traffic violation and discover that the hunt for the "Yorkshire Ripper" is over—or an ordinary citizen will report a ton of pesticides being stored in a warehouse.

In addition, intelligence services around the world constitute a dream environment for narcissists: in fact, I suspect that the level of narcissism is unusually high in such places, because they can (legitimately) break down people into despair (and even torture people, depending upon the country involved). In my opinion an occasional full-page advertisement in all national newspapers encouraging citizens to be observant would probably do far more than any intelligence service in combating domestic terrorism. Surely by now it must be public knowledge that farming pesticides can be used for more things than making crops grow? And that to reasonably purchase a ton of it you should be expected to own at least 1000 acres?

Which brings us to another brand of accomplished narcissist: Pablo Escobar.

Pablo Escobar: Billionaire Cocaine Dealer

When considering the drug trade many people imagine the low-level trader selling hash in a park or pushers in local discos supplying ecstasy or cocaine.

In fact, it's a trillion dollar industry, with most heroin supplies coming from Afghanistan and most cocaine from Columbia. As is well-known, these are both countries seething with wars and unrest: in Columbia alone it can feature anything from Marxist guerrillas selling cocaine to finance their "revolution" to drug lords styling themselves as saviours, as Pablo Escobar did. It can involve everything from individual pushers (often drug users themselves) barely financing their own habit to local drug gangs fighting each other to the death over territory where drug money makes for easy wealth, making them look tough and successful in the eyes of the local kids.

He, because most often it is a he, is slick, smart, a great salesman, and someone who boasts every social skills needed in order to talk with people and befriend them. Whether he's working in a nightclub, bar, pub, social club or any other place where alcohol is consumed he's clever at spotting people who might get a liking for drugs. ("Try this, it'll make you feel great!")

Of course, his prime targets are people with lots of money and the possibility of becoming good regular drug clients, the kind who gather in luxurious nightclubs in London, New York, and Los Angeles or in expensive holiday resorts like Cannes, Malaga and Acapulco. Prostitutes can also make good clients, at least those with plenty of money at hand, because their need for comfort is great and a little encouragement from a drug dealer goes a long way. (The first try might even be free of charge, but the second won't be, that's for sure.)

Here's where the narcissist enjoys drug dealing, knowing full well that drugs can create a lifelong dependency, slowly ruining the user's physical, mental and economic health. What "better" job for someone requiring greater and greater feeling of power, to see people gradually breaking down entirely—not to mention selling them the last batch that finally kills them whether crystalmeth, cocaine or heroin or some hybrid substance once mixed up in a laboratory somewhere else in the world.

The drug trade could very well be the biggest industry in the world: the money is huge. In the US it is estimated that the (illegal) drug trade is as profitable as the six biggest corporations in the country put together. It is possible to make a reasonable living selling and distributing drugs, and with time and personal contacts it's even possible to move up the drug chain and make bigger and bigger deals. A kilo of heroin bought from an Afghan farmer for £2000 could very well bring in over a million pounds in the streets of London after it has been smuggled in and been mixed up and diluted a few times with something like baking powder or brown sugar.

The drug trade is often the foundation on which both local gangs and international cartels flourish, fiercely guarding their territories and their contacts, while feeling nothing but contempt for their victims. It's a perfect environment for the narcissist, despite being, by definition, surrounded by other narcissists. Casual brutality is regarded as normal and natural and even bullying fellow gang members gains what passes for "respect" in a lawless world where police and the law are jointly excluded and narcissistic prey abounds.

Now for a normal loving person, brought up to value honesty and compassion, the drug trade will eventually be too much. Distressed at seeing others' misery, they will probably drop out, or become a victim of drugs themselves. But the malignant narcissist is drawn to the drug trade like moths to the flame: they can never ever have enough of it. The only reason a malignant narcissist would ever pull out is because they've made enough money, they decide that the risk is too great or they are worried about being targeted (often literally) by all their enemies, and choose to move on to other kinds of business. In other words: pure self interest.

Then there are the middlemen, the smugglers themselves, and finally the drug barons like the late Pablo Escobar, who at the peak of his fame, was estimated to be one of the ten wealthiest people in the world.

This is a book about the narcissistic spectrum and Pablo Escobar fits perfectly into this category. His (single) mother was a schoolteacher and he was brought up with many older brothers and sisters. In his brother's book (The Accountant) he relates how bandits came to their area of the country, looting, killing and burning. It was only by sheer luck that they survived—and even then the family were constantly nervous that the bandits would return, forcing them again to barricade the doors, huddle inside and pray. In short, it was an environment likely to give any mother depression and from a young age Pablo Escobar had all the tell-tale trademarks of a malignant narcissist.

After smaller crimes in his youth Escobar became a kidnapper. Nothing gave him more pleasure than to kidnap wealthy people and to extort money from their family—except to sometimes choose to kill the victim whether the ransom was fully paid or not. He took particular pleasure in killing people in front of relatives: from a narcissistic point of view it doubles the joy when not only the victim suffers but the victim's family evidences pure despair as their father, mother, son or daughter is murdered in front of them. Escobar would also sometimes kidnap an entire family and have them killed in order to take over their assets.

It was a lucrative business for Pablo Escobar and only the fact that he became convinced that there was even more money in cocaine made him switch to drugs. The drug trade is of course by definition lawless: when someone owes a few million in uncollected debts there is a well-marked tendency to take the law in one's own hands. In places like northern Mexico or Columbia people can be killed because they owe money or because someone suspects that they talked to the police or simply because another drug lord suspects them of muscling in on his own drug territory. The good thing about the drug trade from the narcissist's standpoint is that you can more or less kill anybody you want and if you enjoy leveling a gun in the face of your victim in order to watch them despair then you can do that too. Professor Robert Hare estimates that as much as 10% of the population is on the narcissistic spectrum, rising in large corporations to as high as 40%, because of the lure of money and narcissistic opportunities. If he's right about large corporations then in the drug trade we can safely assume still higher percentages.

Pablo Escobar would fit well into any or all of our categories. He was motivated by money, to the extent that he became one of the ten wealthiest people on the planet, which makes him a sociopath. His narcissistic credentials are even stronger.

For example, on one occasion he was giving a big pool party in one of his palaces when somebody caught a young boy stealing. Pablo Escobar had the lad tied to a chair and thrown in the swimming pool while he and his guests watched him slowly drown. For Pablo it must have been not only a narcissistic joy to see the boy's struggling to live but also to view his horrified and powerless guests watching it happen, too in awe of Escobar to do anything to stop it.

Of course they did not <u>all</u> wish to save the boy. No doubt most of Pablo's friends would be narcissistic, and in fact they probably had already bonded with him over such "jokes" in the drug trade. No doubt when on their own, they would create exceptionally crude jokes about the boy's hopeless struggle before he drowned: this is how narcissists relate to each other and also identify each other (remember Hitler's chosen few in the private cinema). Whoever said that narcissists lack humour?

Eventually Pablo Escobar had killed so many Columbian policemen, politicians and members of the public that he found his own relatives marked for tit-for-tat retaliation. After a fruitless attempt to reach the highest office in the country the governing party turned on him. Pablo Escobar made a deal that allowed him to build his own prison for himself with billiard tables and swimming pool and every luxury he could think of and he moved in after the deal was made.

Eventually he decided to leave his own prison and "escaped"—if escape is the correct word, since all the guards were on his payroll. However, the Columbian army eventually caught up with him and he was shot dead.

Long after Pablo Escobar's death there was a gripping programme ("Sins of the Fathers") in which Pablo Escobar's son Juan met up with the sons of various top Columbian politicians assassinated by his father. The sons all shook hands and embraced each other in a very moving scene. Now one would expect any son of Pablo Escobar's to be reviled throughout Columbia, but the fact remains that Juan never got involved in the drug trade and doesn't share his father's taste for killing people. The reason for this, I believe, is that Pablo Escobar had married a pretty fifteen-year old girl for her beauty and innocence rather for any narcissistic reason, and, as far as we know, she gave all her children a loving and nurturing upbringing. Therefore the narcissistic circle was broken, despite the genes of Pablo Escobar, the most ruthless drug lord in modern times.

In common with most narcissists Escobar found it hard to understand why so many people got upset with his killings and wanted revenge because he never ever felt any remorse whatsoever. (It is commonly the case that narcissistic people assume that others are just like them.) In the end Pablo Escobar was ruined because too many normal people hated him. Like Hitler, he declared war against too many enemies.

The School Bully

Psychologist Barbara Coloroso, in her excellent book <u>The Bully, the Bullied and the Bystander</u>, points out that bullying is not about anger and conflict but rather about contempt for the victim: that bullying is "arrogance in action". She broadens her argument in <u>Extraordinary Evil</u> where she categorises Adolf Hitler as a bully. All this is true, but the problem still persists as to who becomes a bully, how and why? These questions are what this chapter is about.

So, to return to the narcissistic school bully: statistically speaking, given a normal-sized school class of thirty, there should be at least three children in this category. (Of course in some schools there might be fewer and in others there could be many more.) School is simply the early training ground for the narcissist: what one can do and get away with, how can one mobilize a gang against a victim, how can one spread vicious rumours about the victim in order to mobilize the mob? It's all training for the narcissist's future, whether that future lies in finance in the City of London or as the leader of a Chicago drug gang.

In fact, the school environment, usually involving frequent moves from classroom to classroom and from teacher to teacher (and often involving a number of temporary teachers) can be a dream environment for bullies, who are, without exception, malignant narcissists. Such bullying is systematic, and often planned in advance, with the purpose of breaking the victim down (the more damaged the victim, the more successful the bully). The bully is constantly on the lookout for the unusually sensitive or particularly vulnerable. Such malignant narcissists don't only bully once or twice: they are far more likely to attack the same target over and over again, and even to become addicted to the feeling of power that this gives them.

Bullies can also be surprisingly subtle (sometimes, especially in good schools, they have to be). After all, one generally can't thump someone physically during maths class. In terms of bullying it's much safer to spread horrible rumours about a person, perhaps someone depressive, poor or homosexual: the possibilities here are endless. The leader can then do the background work and little by little communicate with others, and once enough bullies have gathered they can attack the victim together—often after a lengthy build-up, raising the prospect of attacks on the victim, and thus arousing dread and panic pleasurable to the sadists if horrible for the victim.

Once a pattern of bullying has been established and the victim has become too terrified to complain or to ask for help the bully will rise to still greater efforts. Often he won't release his grip until the victim breaks down, stays away from school, changes school or—in extreme cases—is driven to suicide. Other students are almost always too intimidated to intervene, while teachers can't see what happens outside school, or on busses—not to mention in school dressing rooms or toilets. These days cyberbullying and even cyberblackmail are the latest ways whereby narcissists can refine pure cruelty into an art form.

Show me a bully and I will show you a narcissist. The schools are mainly his happy hunting-ground, allowing the bully not only to hone their bullying skills but, most importantly, to learn how to blame others and get away with it. Take for example the bully, hauled in to explain himself to the school head, who explains that "it was all an innocent game". Such people move on bullying school-mates to bullying colleagues in whatever occupation they work in. (I believe that some occupations are more gratifying than others for narcissists, especially those giving automatic power over others. See the chapter on "The Narcissist at Work".)

Basically the school-age narcissist fine-tunes techniques to be used later on in life, including how to pick victims and how best to break them down, whether it is selecting someone supremely vulnerable or because they happen to be in the way with regard to further advancement in society, work or business. To backstab work colleges will often lead to faster advancement (as described in Oliver James' <u>Office Politics</u>), while sabotaging others' work is not only commonplace but also often difficult to prove.

I should also stress that narcissistic bullying has almost nothing in common with teasing. One can call someone "Fatty" or "Thicko" for years, even thousands of times, with some level of acceptance and even affection. There is no affection at all in the cold-blooded selection of a victim likely to break down in tearful despair—even possibly someone likely to commit suicide, to the narcissistic delight of the bully. (Choosing his victim is an intuitive skill that the serious narcissist develops: it's crucial that he chooses a victim whom he can break.)

The most modern version of school bullying is cyberbullying, where vicious things are suggested about a victim on social websites such as Facebook or Twitter, which can go viral and even reach thousands of people. (Such websites are notoriously lax about allowing "free speech" at any price.)

Cyberbullying and cyberblackmail are both very worrying and relatively recent, giving the narcissist newish ways of spreading misery. In fact, to consider bullying or cyberbullying without mentioning narcissism is like writing a serious book about swimming but somehow failing to mention that it involves contact with water. There may be other factors: socio-economic, racist, drugs etc., but narcissism is always the main one.

School bullying, even in its most serious form, has always existed, but there are signs that it's going underground and also becoming more sophisticated, in a culture where intimidation and beatings can be put on the internet for "fun" (presumably in order to amuse fellow-narcissists, since no normal person could enjoy them). Every year young people all over the world commit suicide and sometimes such tragedies are clearly related to bullying, on or off the "net". However, most often the reasons are not clear-cut and such tragedies can also happen many years later—which doesn't mean that bullying narcissists played no part, only that the ultimate reaction can be built up over a long period of time.

"Happy slapping" is slang for when a gang attacks somebody, perhaps in the street or a corridor, or maybe in a school bathroom. The difference between this and normal assault is that the gang not only brutally assault their victim but also <u>film the whole event</u> on their mobile phones, later sharing it among themselves in order to more fully enjoy the moment when somebody got beaten, injured or knocked out.

There is no evidence that bullying has decreased over the decades. On the contrary, it is almost certainly on the increase, especially as teachers are increasingly wary of interfering, since bullies can often turn the tables such that the teacher becomes their next victim. In these cases car tires are mysteriously slashed, abusive phone calls occur in the middle of the night or mysterious postings appear on websites regarding the teacher's presumed sexual preferences or similar degrading forms of abuse. Many teachers are in 2013(rightly) petrified of their pupils and for a teacher to be bullied is not uncommon.

Therefore school itself becomes only a practice ground for bullies, a place where they learn what they can get away with. Bullying is a skill that malignant narcissists learn and develop—a sadistic skill they can spend a lifetime perfecting, and all because they have no empathy in their brains.

At the risk of belaboring the point, a narcissist is not (repeat not) a normal, well-meaning person. Instead he learns how to give the illusion of being a model citizen, while all the time seeking narcissistic prey (the rest of us)—while a school bully is usually a completely formed narcissist honing his or her skills for bigger and better opportunities later on in life.

Osama Bin Laden And Al-Qaeda

The Soviet Union's war in Afghanistan (1979-1989) became a major contributing factor towards that country's economic collapse, draining the country's resources with huge debts and foreign loans, and indirectly assisting to bankrupt the Soviet Union. One of its less-noticed disadvantages, however, was in bringing Osama bin Laden, riddled with hatred of the Soviets, to join the Afghani Taliban. Bin Laden's personal role was to assist the Afghani Taliban in financing and organising the war against the Soviet Union (which also proved to be hugely bloody, costing almost a million Afghan lives).

After the Soviet Union finally pulled out, the Taliban (with Bin Laden and Al-Qaeda's approval) transformed this once-beautiful country into an old-fashioned Muslim state where women had to wear burqas from top to toe and every other aspect of fundamentalist Islam was ardently enforced. Ancient and beautiful statues were blown up because they were portraits of women (or indeed of religious men). Much music was banned: history rewritten.

It must have felt very much like Nazi Germany in the 1930s, especially as, after an internal weeding out of any resistance, totalitarianism was gradually introduced. And just as Nazi Germany turned bitterly against their old allies in the Soviet Union after the non-aggression pact of 1939, the Taliban and Al-Qaeda turned in hatred against their previous benefactor: the USA.

In Germany it was the grief and defeat of WWI, the hyperinflation directly after the war and the 1929 stock market crash that created a population with perhaps as many as 50% of mothers with postnatal depression—ripe to eventually support somebody like Adolf Hitler. In Afghanistan by contrast it was the long drawn-out war against the Soviets, including hardship and financial misery, which created another generation of hugely depressed mothers. They gave birth to sons who relished the idea of violence and revenge, who rushed to support the Taliban and to join Al-Qaeda—not to mention fighting in the Afghan war that still meanders on. (One unforgettable—some would say unforgiveable—memory of many Americans and Europeans is Pakastanis dancing in the streets in celebration of 9/11.)

We can also view the Taliban and Al-Qaeda as criminal enterprises, financed by heroin in the same way as Columbian Marxist guerrillas were financed by cocaine. It is pure "narcissistic logic" to give people the illusion that they're in a political organization when in fact they're simply supporting a criminal enterprise.

And then there are links between narcissistic terrorists. Ireland's IRA on the one hand was a supposedly Marxist liberation front and on the other hand a criminal gang of thugs demanding protection money from small Irish businesses while controlling the Northern Ireland drug trade. It was James Monaghan, Martin McCaule and Niall Connelly from the IRA who taught Marxist guerrillas in Columbia how to blow up buildings more efficiently. (Any excuse to cause despair.)

The same narcissistic reasoning can be applied to Osama bin Laden and Al-Qaeda. They moved from loathing the Soviet Union to weeding out local resistance inside Afghanistan, and (when they run out of local victims) they simply turned on their former supporters, the Americans, creating the catastrophe of 9/11.

Thus we will continue to see the Taliban and Al-Qaeda assuring their supporters that theirs is really a religious struggle, and that they are not a heroin-based enterprise at all. As long as there are good heroin harvests in Afghanistan there will be an active Taliban because they can not only send Westerners into heroin addiction but also make money to support their violence—what a narcissistic cocktail! Of course, Osama Bin Laden is now dead, but I wonder whether his poisonous legacy might not prove to be, first to break up the Soviet Union—and then to break the USA.

Perhaps one of the best explanations of why Bin Laden became Bin Laden can be found in the book by his sister-in-law Carmen Bin Laden, <u>The Wild Kingdom</u>. For some reason Osama Bin Laden's mother was not only divorced but was even shunned by her husband after his birth. She had to live with the shame of becoming an outcast in the (enormous and also enormously rich) Bin Laden family after Osama was born. I have no doubt that this would have given her and indeed any woman who cared about the fate of her children, severe postnatal depression.

It was fascinating to learn, after the military raid in Pakistan when Osama Bin Laden was shot, that he was filmed watching the video of 9/11 and the collapse of the World Trade Center towers—not just once, but over and over again, with a joy that only fellow narcissists could watch without disbelief.

It was called the World Trade Center because companies from all over the world were based there: indeed, 373 foreign nationals from 60 countries died on 9/11, not counting those with dual nationality. It's certainly fair to say that Bin Laden wasn't too fussy about whom he murdered. In New York, at least, it would have been hard to kill more foreigners unless he had actually targeted the headquarters of the United Nations.

Al-Qaeda's goal is simply to move the world back to how it was when their religion was founded, around 1300 years ago. Therefore a barber who dares to use an electric hair trimmer can be regarded as a legitimate target simply because electric hair trimmers did not exist during the time of the prophet Mohammed: many barbers in Afghanistan and Pakistan have thus been decapitated. This is of course an excellent example of the "narcissistic logic" that the Afghans have to live with. The same can be said about girls and women attending schools and universities: to such terrorists, females traveling to and from school comprise "legitimate" targets.

Just as Hitler watched "snuff" films of executions and hangings, Osama Bin Laden surely received unmeasurable pleasure from watching the World Trade Center disintegrate, from hearing the screams and from seeing the horror from the fleeing bystanders—not to mention the utter despair of the people trapped in the towers (or imagining that of those—still worse—trapped in the planes).

I have no doubt that every (aggressive) participant during 9/11 was a narcissist and that it gave each of them an astonishing "kick" to kill people. But not every narcissist is a murderer. We'll now consider the narcissist you've almost certainly already met: the narcissist at work.

The Narcissist At Work

Certain jobs suit the warped tastes of those on the narcissistic spectrum especially well. For example, managerial jobs, the kind where hirings and firings are not scrutinised—or else jobs in companies where employees never quite manage to "fit in" unless they're narcissists themselves. Also jobs including police, prison guards or security guards (for the most damaged of these, to torment or jail an innocent person must be the ultimate narcissistic treat). Not to mention imagining how the victim might react when the jury foreman declares him "guilty". There are also interrogation tapes to be gloated over, and even to be shared with similarly narcissistic colleagues (see "How Hitler became Hitler".)

Various inspectors working for government bodies can also have a "field day" at work. Imagine an Inland Revenue Inspector who has simply set his mind on nailing one taxpayer and who investigates to such a degree that his victim commits suicide. This I believe is not unheard-of, and yet such rigorous investigation can be seen as something normal, and even praiseworthy.

Other occupations give the malignant narcissist better opportunities than others in order to achieve dominance and control. Positions including prison guards, police, prosecutors, managers, doctors and even psychiatrists are all examples of jobs where authority figures are unlikely to be questioned—as long as they choose the right victim to "break". For example, his profession certainly served Dr Shipman well: even when denounced as a possible murderer, people were reluctant to believe it of a kindly-looking local GP. While any number of malevolent psychiatrists can theoretically "break" a patient Shipman was able to murder his, by simply saying that the patient "got worse", "got weaker" or "died of old age".

Working as a psychiatrist or psychoanalyst the malignant narcissist can really get under the skin of his victim and—if that client breaks down— perhaps he or she had an underlying mental illness that floated up to the surface during therapy. More research needs to be done into the power that analysts possess (in terms of bullying alone) in their relationships with clients.

Few occupations have been riddled with killers to the same degree as medicine and psychology. It's not merely that Ted Bundy studied psychology, probably there learning how to charm his many victims—or that Dr Harold Shipman learned how to cajole older women into a fatal dose of morphine. Psychology as a subject actually gets it wrong because mental illness is imagined to come, "out of a blue sky" rather than being created by a narcissistic environment.

It isn't hard to see how a victim of internet stalking, for example, could have spent years (even decades) in psychotherapy without having ever have figured out that it was just one narcissistic person behind it all. Since Professor Robert Hare estimates approximately 5% of most populations to be narcissists (with an additional 4% to be sociopaths and 1% psychopaths) it isn't hard to imagine that some proportion of depressed or even schizophrenic illness might well be a direct result of induced mental disorder.

Or, to put it in plain and simple English, the very presence of narcissists <u>creates</u> other mental illnesses.

As has already been mentioned, Ted Bundy studied psychology (and indeed worked as a psychologist in a call center, where people could phone in regarding their personal problems). It is clear that psychotherapy, where the therapist sits as a God-like figure, with full permission to dig into the mind of "the patient", is a dream job for a narcissist where they can witness the despair in the patient, and even contribute (if they desire) to tipping the patient over the edge. (Should this occur, it could always be explained in medical journals as "the patient had underlying depression and schizophrenia that only emerged during the therapy sessions".)

There are two main problems in psychology today, as I perceive it. The first is that the "patient" in therapy suffering depression or schizophrenia might very well have received this from a narcissistic person close to the "patient" (whether in the past or in the present) while psychology would mainly imagine that the depression or schizophrenia came down like lightning out of a clear sky. It might be a death in the family or financial difficulties, underlying years of mental abuse or some other reason that is the underlying real cause for the depression.

The main reason why psychology fails is that the therapist him or herself can sometimes find narcissistic delight in the patient's despair, which will of course not only fail to help the patient recover but sometimes make his condition worse. As I write, there are no checks as to whether a psychologist, psychotherapist or psychiatrist might be narcissistic and, as such, unsuitable to give therapy (whether they might benefit themselves from it is another matter).

As far as I know there is no reason for medical doctors or psychiatrists to undergo any kind of test to establish if they have narcissistic tendencies (although there <u>are</u> exhaustive tests for anyone hoping to work with children, in order to find out or if they have any possible background as a child molester or paedophile).

Therefore if a psychiatrist wrongly comes to the conclusion in therapy that the patient had "underlying depression or schizophrenia" that "surfaced during psychotherapy" then they get away with it (even were the patient to commit suicide) because this is what narcissistic people do. Narcissistic people take great joy in breaking down people and if they can send their victims into despair and depression (even schizophrenia, in especially vulnerable people) they will do so with great enthusiasm.

And so: How many psychiatrists fit into the narcissistic category? We just don't know, but personally I believe there are rather more than in the general population because of the money, power and endless possibilities to manipulate patients' emotions—and still to get away with it.

But not only psychoanalysts. In the corporate world managers are regularly allowed to hire and fire people at will, often using this power to bully people on a daily basis until they can bear it no more and leave. It's hugely easy to label an employee as "incompetent" and fire them. Often no proof is required, and rather than face the stress and expense of going to court the bullied employee often simply starts looking for another job, hoping against hope for better luck elsewhere.

Malignant narcissists head most big corporations, which can surprise no one. However, in some companies the culture itself is narcissistic, and if you don't happen to be that way inclined you would never fit in (examples include Enron, Arthur Andersen, WorldCom and Lehman Brothers). So if you enjoy looking down on your competitors, have a low opinion of other corporations compared to yours and relish tormenting people beneath you in the corporate structure then there is a reasonable chance that you are a happily employed corporate narcissist, fitting perfectly into your organisation: a dream job!

However, it's crucial to recall that the bully at work usually also has a family life, where his partner, and perhaps even their children, represent fair game. By constantly demanding things from their children, even youngsters can be made to feel innately inferior, a small series of miseries capable of being achieved on a daily basis. As for the bully, his/her goals include the following: Never praise your own children, always point out their shortcomings, consistently compare them to other ("better") children and should they—against all odds—manage to succeed at anything, then be sure to attack them for something else (untidiness, schoolwork, lack of creativity, etc.)

Interestingly, in his book <u>The Wisdom of Psychopaths</u>, Dr. Kevin Dutton (Magdalen College, Oxford) lists the most "psychopathic" occupations as follows:

1) CEO
2) Lawyer
3) Media representative (TV/Radio)
4) Salesperson
5) Surgeon
6) Journalist
7) Police Officer
8) Cleric
9) Chef
10) Civil Servant.

It isn't difficult to see how such lethal combinations of money and power could influence a psychopath's occupational choices (though the "cleric" is, these days, rather surprising).

They surround us in our daily lives today.

1938 Nazi Kristallnacht, Riots In London 2011 And Stockholm 2013

After the deadly shooting of Londoner Mark Duggan (April 2011) because a few policemen "believed" that he was carrying a gun, rioting broke out in Tottenham, later spreading to other parts of London and well beyond. Two other people also died, while houses and cars were set on fire, windows were smashed, and shops looted. Eventually, after the rioting had spread as far as Birmingham and Nottingham, around 3000 people were arrested and many later convicted. Police response to the unrest was later adjudged, "too few, too slow, and too timid" and eventually it was heavy rain that contributed to the end of days of the English riots. (Obviously Mark Duggan's death meant little or nothing to most of the rioters. It simply became an excuse for anybody to join in.)

It's not hard to see a connection to Kristallnacht in 1938 Germany, where synagogues and Jewish shops where set on fire or plundered, their glass windows shattered, giving the riot its incongruously lovely name: crystal night or Kristallnacht.

What the English riots have in common with the Nazi Kristallnacht is narcissistic joy. For the narcissist it's not only a pleasure to seize (for example) electrical goods without paying for them, but especially to see or imagine the despair and utter helplessness in the faces of the shop owners when windows are smashed, shops looted, hopes ruined and property set on fire. It has been often suggested that it was Goebbels' propaganda that "conned" normal law-abiding Germans to riot during Kristallnacht, but for a narcissist the merest hint that it's temporarily acceptable to smash windows, plunder or set fire to buildings will be more than sufficient encouragement. The same can be said about London, where the word soon spread that "the police did wrong so it's OK to riot", even if over 99% of the rioters could never have known Mark Duggan and were merely seeking an excuse. The notion that the English riots were somehow based on poverty or race (what about all the white rioters?) is as mistaken as saying that the Jews in Nazi Germany were targeted on Kristallnacht because they were all wealthy, just because some Jews were well-off. There's no <u>real</u> logic behind narcissistic behaviour: only "narcissistic logic".

Unfortunately for narcissists after many centuries of "good times" people are beginning to recognise narcissism for what it is. The purpose of this book is primarily to make future life for narcissistic people more difficult, and to make their warped logic harder for normal people to accept.

Strangely enough in Stockholm, not long after the London shooting, there was a similar shooting that also resulted in days of looting, burning and smashing of cars. Now anybody who has lived in Sweden (and most who have not) know that there social benefits are generous, and that, although police are armed, the guidelines involving their use of firearms are very restrictive. Yet all this failed to stop some young narcissists from believing that the 1917 October revolution had returned and that anarchy was again the norm, while stealing and burning is acceptable as long as some political justification can be imagined to exist.

To be blunt, all narcissists, sociopaths and psychopaths are rotten to the core and society at large would be far better off without them. For this reason alone, it should be any civilised society's long-term goal to have as few mothers suffer postnatal depression as possible—and not only because most suffer in silence. Ten years onward it creates a new generation of school bullies; twenty years beyond it creates the new group of criminals; and thirty years on it creates misery and ruin in workplaces, corporations and even the world (and this is all without reference to murder).

Goodwin, Rbs And The Profit Vacuum

Lately we've had any number of spectacular bankruptcies in the business world. Corporations including Lehman Brothers, WorldCom, RBS and Enron have all gone to the wall, not to mention the collapse of the accounting firm Arthur Andersen, plus a long list of fraudulent "Ponzi" schemes like Bernhard Madhoff's. The list is too long and the subject too huge to fully explore in this book (it will be thoroughly investigated in a further book). However, it's certainly fair to say that business theory consistently ignores the fact that the principal reasons for corporate failure are narcissism, sociopathy and psychopathy.

It's amazing that in 2013, despite a string of corporate failures, Professor Robert Hare can still assert that 40% of those employed in larger corporations belong to the group of either narcissists, sociopaths, or psychopaths.

There is nothing in my professional experience as an IT consultant that would contradict Hare in any way. In fact I would even claim that in some companies you couldn't possibly fit in to the management structure unless you were somewhere on the narcissistic spectrum, while in sales departments for some (very large) corporations the true figure could be above 80%.

Similarly, at least to my knowledge, there exists no economic theory capable of handling what happens when a narcissist comes to power in a country and recklessly spends government money (not to mention approving reckless government borrowing) in order to be re-elected, eventually to leave the country in utter financial ruin. In short we have moved from "Ponzi" businesses to "Ponzi" economies, where a couple of hundred people whose only goal was to be re-elected are prepared to spend money as if it rained down from heaven, and all they had to do was to scoop it up and spend it. In Europe it has been mostly primarily socialist parties (run by narcissists) that have subjected countries including Greece, Spain, Italy, Portugal, France and Great Britain into a huge debt liability for generations to come, though the conservatives are not guiltless either.

In the USA the following factors that put the US into a staggering debt area of $17 trillion: a lethal combination of enormous defense spending on wars including Iraq and Afghanistan, the maintenance of over 130 foreign military bases, enormously expensive military hardware such as the stealth bomber, plus the combination of enormous tax cuts and social welfare spending.

This level of debt will surely drag down the world economy for generations to come—and all because some narcissistic politicians couldn't care less about the debt burden left behind for future generations. (This will be more thoroughly examined in the next book, where we will see the effect of narcissism and the "manna theory".) In this chapter we'll concentrate on business narcissists, specifically on Fred Goodwin and RBS.

Now in business generally, firing people who aren't part of your own inner circle and replacing them with people who are is standard practice, with or without financial incentive (though that can be considerable).

For example in a large software project (employing perhaps over 100 developers) it does not take a genius to figure out that 75% commission on top of $100,000 multiplied by 100 people will mount up to a juicy $7.5 million in commission: well worth backstabbing competitors for. People have after all been murdered for less (especially in drug-dealing) so some daily backstabbing is regarded amongst the average narcissistic project participant as "no big deal" because after all "they only have themselves to blame".

If we look at RBS the real figures involved thousands of employees and contractors outsourced beyond RBS, while Deloitte and Touche claim 75% in commissions for them. I would not be surprised if we weren't talking about perhaps 10,000 people inside RBS with a direct or indirect link to Deloitte. The truth is that we simply do not know.

After all, Deloitte and Touche didn't recommend Fred Goodwin to RBS because they considered him such a great guy. Fred Goodwin was part of

Deloitte, he was "their man" in RBS, and because he failed so abysmally Deloitte are to some degree responsible for his actions. I feel sure, as do many people, that there's a connection between the size of the invoices from Deloitte and all the people they placed in RBS (not to mention the bank's eventual failure and public bailout). As for ABN Amro: that was just the cream on the cake. In fact RBS is just one example of what happens when too many people in the top lose connection with reality and believe in their own narcissistic power.

The official story is that Fred Goodwin proved to be an efficient CEO in many companies before reaching the Royal Bank of Scotland. He had certainly cultivated a reputation for being ruthless at cost-cutting and for being his own man, as well as awarding himself huge salaries and enormous bonuses. There are just no business theories to assist with analyzing somebody like Fred Goodwin because words like narcissism and sociopath are excluded—at least, not in any text that I know of.

Modern business theory prefers to use words like "structural change", "re-engineering", "organizational layering" and so on. When did we last read that "Enron failed because the top management and board were, almost without exception, sociopaths"? Or: "Certain European states have endured a recent history of narcissistic leaders too desperate to retain power to care about the size of the country's debt they left behind them"?

So let's glance at ex-Sir Fred Goodwin's career. First Deloitte and Touche groomed him for the RBS job. They would be commissioned to write reports about company management, the reports being sent to the company board. In their analyses, Deloitte would normally complain as much as they dared about the existing CEO, even at times recommending a new CEO, until they got the person they wanted in control. (Behind the scenes they might well have gone still farther, painting anyone not connected with them as useless, and campaigning hard for his or her removal with the Board.) In some cases the CEO would indeed be removed and Deloitte would submit "their man" Fred Goodwin in his or her place (n.b. Goodwin had first become a partner in Deloitte in 1988).

In this fashion Goodwin became CEO of Short Brothers, in Northern Ireland, in 1989, Clydesdale Bank (after a takeover) and Yorkshire Bank in 1995, also after a takeover. He joined the Royal Bank of Scotland as a deputy CEO in 1998 and worked there as CEO from 2001-2008 during which time they took over NatWest, First Active, Churchill Insurance, and Direct Line, not to mention the USA's Citizen Financial Group, Charter One Financial Inc. and eventually the Dutch bank ABN Amro.

In short, Fred Goodwin while at RBS bought a new company almost every year up to 2004, when there was a modest gap of three years until the takeover of ABN Amro. At each company he took every chance he could of firing people on the flimsiest possible grounds, replacing them with people from Deloitte and Touche.

There is an expression amongst accountants that some corporations that go out of business "expand themselves to death". We will now see how Goodwin's greed permitted this to happen.

During my years in IT and accounting I've seen a large number of new system installations, mostly of course moving from manual routines to computerised ones. Accountancy jobs are of small fry in comparison with all the consultancy work that can be outsourced to Deloitte (including IT work, management consulting and project work: although I don't have the figures my guess is that Deloitte's total work per year for RBS could very well amount to hundreds of millions per year).

And yet what Goodwin did was no more than what generally happens when narcissists come to power: to fire employees, creating a lucrative vacuum that they (or Deloitte) can then can fill up with their own people, along with contractors that they can put on their payroll (for a fat fee, of course). Management theory suggests that one should fire the non-productive or incompetent, but, as we have seen, in reality extant employees are more likely to give way to external consultancy on a high payroll. It's rather a fight over who controls the payroll, taking any excuse possible to get rid of somebody on the wrong payroll.

So who was fired under Goodwin? First, anybody who dared to hint that it might not be in RBS' interest to give so much contract work to Deloitte: secondly, anybody who complained about Goodwin. We can see how the RBS under Goodwin gradually came to be more and more tightly run by Deloitte. RBS' expansion benefited Deloitte directly as well, because they won juicy project contracts.

From Fred Goodwin's point of view it was a narcissistic bonanza. People who had spent a lifetime in the bank, who had worked themselves up through the company hierarchy over years comprise wonderful narcissistic prey—because, of course, they have that much more to lose.

One wrong smile, one wrong word, one wrong gesture: this was enough. Fred Goodwin ruled by fear, and nobody dared to criticize his words or actions (or his purchasing of other corporations, such as ABN Amro). In the end it seemed to be as simple as that Goodwin would fire people for being on the wrong payroll. That meant that if you are paid directly by RBS your chances of survival were slight (because Deloitte made no commission on you) whereas if you were working through Deloitte and some profit adhered to Deloitte you were far likelier to be safe. (Once Hitler rose to power, within a few years every German police station was controlled by the Gestapo. It's hard not to imagine that any local police chief that objected would be fired: some reason would be invented as to why he "wasn't right" for the job. This is an exact parallel to what happened to many RBS managers once Fred Goodwin took over.)

This is not unheard-of in IT work, where being on the right payroll can be far more important than doing a good job. Fascinatingly it's also completely normal using "narcissistic logic", where a conspiracy can be built up against almost anybody for almost any reason at all, and from a narcissistic point of view it's a principal topic of discussion most of the time. This means not only finding fault in the "victim" but also building up a conspiracy against them, where almost no exaggeration can be too outrageous. (This backstabbing is of course also a bonding activity between narcissists.) So in RBS your job would only be safe if, firstly, you're on Deloitte and Touche's payroll, and secondly, if you vigorously contribute to smear campaigns against those fellow employees who are on the "wrong" payroll. It is basically corporate bullying. (Once you have built up a case against a fellow employee and eventually managed to get the person fired then you just simply move on to the next narcissistic victim and and start a new campaign.)

There was a hiatus from 2004 to 2007, when ABN Amro was bought, during which period Fred Goodwin was clearly desperate to make RBS into one of the largest banks in the world, with all the fame and power that this would give him. At that time I suspected that the US house market would sink (ABN Amro had large stakes in the US property market). Had Deloitte done their homework it would have been obvious that this was likely. There were also many excellent books predicting a massive fall in the sub-prime US property market. (I owned three of these personally.) Had Goodwin not been so avaricious for personal gain as to grab company after company—and had he not such narcissistic need to fire at will whomever he disliked—the disastrous ABN Amro deal might have been avoided. A good captain always knows when it's time to out-run the incoming storm: Goodwin didn't.

ABN Amro had basically become a tipping ground for American salesmen who needed a garbage dump in order to rid themselves of their sub-prime mortgage disasters: they found the fool they sought in ABN Amro. All this is fairly basic, and one would have thought that a CEO earning over £100 million per year might have known it.

Finally, we can only speculate as to why Goodwin paid for ABN Amro with RBS cash rather than with shares. It's hard not to imagine that he thought paying with shares would dilute the share value of his multitude of personally-held RBS shares. (As for Deloitte, of course, the purchase of ABN Amro would mean a bonanza of consultancies and projects.)

Shortly after RBS bought ABN Amro we heard how Lehman Brothers, after borrowing no less than 43 times the value of their actual assets, went out of business, rocking the stockmarket, while the rest of the world crashed.

In the end the rules should be changed such that banks can't become so big that they have to be bailed out by governments. Public opinion these days is shifting towards smaller banks that can safely fail without government intervention. However, Deloitte remains the accountants for RBS, where presumably they daily pray that Mr Goodwin will continue in hiding, perhaps in a mansion in France, keeping his blinds down. Because if it could be proven that Deloitte and Touche had advised Goodwin to take over ABN Amro then it is far from inconceivable that we might see Deloitte being obliged to compensate angry RBS shareholders and (just like Arthur Andersen under similar circumstances) cease to exist overnight.

But the welfare of RBS was never Goodwin's main concern: he was more interested in finding a new supply of narcissistic prey. Or perhaps he was worried that paying for ABN Amro with shares would dilute his own RBS private stock options? At any rate he paid cash: a move that sealed destiny, both for him and for RBS. (Of course, none of the narcissistic yes-men with which Fred Goodwin had deliberately surrounded himself would have objected to the ABN Amro takeover. It is part of the narcissistic personality—see Saddam Hussein, the locked door and the reading out of the names of those "traitors" to his cause—that any kind of criticism is perceived as deceitfulness or worse.)

As for Goodwin, I believe his narcissism irresistibly impelled him towards getting his hands on ABN Amro. The takeover (albeit briefly) made him the CEO of the world's largest bank, with all the pay, perks and share options commensurate with such a position—though I still wonder whether perhaps it was the opportunity to go in to ABN Amro and fire people at will that was the biggest narcissistic motivation. Having said which, Goodwin's greed might well have impacted on many more victims than all his firings did... RBS shares fell in 2008 from almost £7 per share to just two pence per share and the British government had to bail them out by buying up 80% of the shares. Today (April 2012) RBS shares are hovering around 25 pence: millions of RBS employees and investors lost money because of Fred Goodwin's sociopathic greed.

Professor Robert Hare has devised an excellent test, which, if implemented in law, would identify those on the narcissistic spectrum. If such a test was imposed and those who failed it ruled out from positions of corporate leadership it would probably do far more than any legislation to reform the banks! (But then, which banker could possibly manage to pass it?)

What we can say in general is that narcissist, sociopaths and psychopaths are drawn to large corporations as cockroaches are drawn to food cabinets, because of money and power and a constant fresh supply of narcissistic victims who will break down when they are fired.

We can also suggest a theory as to how large corporations collapse. Let's say that in a "normal" large corporation there are 40% narcissistic, sociopathic and psychopathic high-level employees (not excluding the company board). When the narcissistic level increases beyond this, already far exaggerated, point then eventually reality will go out of the window. We can only speculate (to use the favourite buzzword) where the "tipping point" might be, in terms of top management, but, wherever it is, it was certainly well exceeded at RBS.

The Failed Milgram Experiment

Yale University psychologist Stanley Milgram conducted his eponymous experiment in 1961, over a three-month period. Inspired by the Adolf Eichmann trial, Milgram hoped to show that anybody could "become evil", under certain stimuli and psychological pressures.

First Milgram advertised in the Yale local press for "high-paid temporary jobs", attracting hundreds of potential applicants.

His experiment involved the following: a man (who was an actor, although this was unknown to the applicants) was bound to what appears to be an electric chair, with its cables connected. There was a glass window between the actor and the applicant: before the latter was a switchboard supposedly capable of giving the actor electric shocks from 1 to 450 volts. A "leader" dressed in a white medical coat supervised the experiment.

The whole point was to fool the applicant. S/he was told to read out questions to the actor: idiotic questions often, or questions with no right answer. Whenever the actor got the answer "wrong" the applicant was instructed to give him an electric shock, with the dosage increasing with each wrong answer. The crucial point was this: the applicant had no notion that the man in the chair was merely acting and that no electric shocks were actually administered. The core of the experiment was to test how many people were prepared to go over the 450 volt mark which—had the electricity voltage been real—would have killed the actor. Meantime experiment leaders in white coats walked around, ordering the innocent applicants to continue the experiment.

Milgram's original surmise was that only a couple of psychopaths would be willing to administer the full 450 volts: but, in the event, the result was hugely different. Instead, 65% of the subjects proved willing to carry out the maximum 450 volt electric shock when ordered to do so by men in medical coats. Milgram therefore concluded that almost any normal person can do evil when told to obey by a figure in authority. This finding proved hugely controversial, even after a later experiment produced a strikingly similar result.

But there remain three big problems with the experiment, in my opinion. First of all it occurred in 1961: only sixteen years after WWII ended. Students at Yale University would be aged from 17 to 24, and many would have been born during the war. Still worse, many wives and girlfriends lost their partners during the war and could very well have suffered postnatal depression.

Therefore in 1961 it is only reasonable to expect that there would be a much higher proportion of narcissists, sociopaths and psychopaths in the chosen age group than would generally be the norm during peacetime—indeed, it might even have touched 20%-25% among the younger generation.

The second serious flaw in Milgram's experiment is that an "easy and well-paid" job is likely to attract a higher proportion of applicants who are narcissists, sociopaths and psychopaths than normal people (particularly sociopaths, who are money-driven).

The third difficulty is that a higher degree of narcissists, sociopaths and psychopaths are drawn to attend university—any university, though perhaps particularly Ivy League—because a university degree is still supposed to guarantee a higher income and greater opportunities to be put in positions of power, where others might be used as narcissistic prey. Professor Robert Hare has demonstrated that in large corporations there are up to four times as many psychopaths in top corporations as the equivalent number of employees in small businesses, because there's bigger money combined with a greater chance to target narcissistic prey. While Yale—through its very distinction—is probably home to a good deal more than most.

Thus I believe the experiment to be fatally flawed. Because, although it became world-famous, it failed to differentiate between "normal" people and the narcissists, sociopaths and psychopaths who would be unlikely to feel any compunction about harming others, making the whole purpose of the experiment pointless. Milgram thought that "people are people" and that an actor barking orders wearing a white doctor's coat could make the difference. The flaw in his thinking however is that not everybody is alike—or even "normal".

We can only speculate as to how many narcissists, sociopaths and psychopaths would have given the lethal-level dose of electric shock, but I suspect it could be over 90%. Equally it would be fascinating to know the proportion of non-narcissists who would go so far as to administer an electric shock capable of killing an innocent person. (No doubt one or two might become sufficiently confused to administer a supposedly lethal electric shock but we may never know.) I believe that what Milgram's experiment really showed is that a high number of narcissistic people applied for an "easy, well-paid" job, and because Milgram failed to differentiate between them and normal people his experiment is at best flawed and at worst useless.

Indeed, the experiment may be as pointless as it is famous. When will we ever see a Milgram experiment where a psychopathic test is first applied to each and anybody offered the chance to administer a supposedly serious electric shock? Probably never: perhaps it's simply too frightening to recognise that over 10% of the population aren't normal, especially considering that there's no "cure" apart from locking them up—which is no cure at all.

A New View: Psychologist Oliver Psychologist Oliver James

Oliver James is perhaps currently the UK's most famous child psychologist, publishing best-sellers including They F*** You Up: how to survive family life, How Not to F*** Them Up, and Office Politics: How to Thrive in a World of Lying, Backstabbing and Dirty Tricks.

In this chapter I intend to focus on Oliver James' How Not to F*** Them Up. As a child psychologist, his main theme here is that a child is far better off during the first three years of age in the care of a single adult (ideally, the mother). His point is that nursery and day-care provide less than maternal-level care and that, after the mother, any of the following: father, grandparents, relatives or older siblings, will provide far better child-care than nursery or day-care providers.

According to Oliver James, a child under the age of three doesn't need to play with other children, due to the obvious potential conflicts over toys, plus territorial disputes. His research suggests that children in this age-group play "in parallel", integrating for less than two or three minutes on average: in short, they're too young to truly relate to each other during play. In addition, children under three don't need teachers: instead they need to be looked after. Day-care centres are bad places for toddlers in this age-band, creating constant stress (proven by a higher level of measurable cortisol in such toddlers).

Oliver James divides mothers into three categories:

1) "The Organiser". This kind of mother believes that the baby needs to be controlled as soon as possible because s/he otherwise will become indulged,

selfish and naughty. Potty training and sleeping routines are implemented as soon as possible in order to fit in with the mother's work schedules. Perhaps 25% of UK mothers belong to this group, where full-time work for the mother is the norm. Organisers are mostly professional women, already accustomed to a well-run work environment—and who try to organise their families in a similar fashion. An <u>extreme</u> Organiser might put in a baby into nursery when the child is only three months old, in order to rush back to work. A <u>wealthy</u> Organiser might instead employ au-pairs, hoping that they will do a good job for the baby. In both cases, breastfeeding and close bonding end sooner rather than later in order to fit in with work schedules. (Organisers sometimes consider being at home as dull compared with a more stimulating work environment, and can be controlling towards their baby.) There are even higher risks for Organisers who are unemployed with a newborn and unable to find work. Interrupted sleep is an important factor (and/or a feeling of hopelessness and not be able to cope because of irregular feeding patterns).

2) "The Hugger" by contrast places the baby's needs before everything else. Often she is a full-time mother at home, where hugging her child is a priority. In most countries, around 25% of mothers are full-time mothers. The hugger adapts her schedule to the baby's, regarding breastfeeding and sleep patterns.

3) "The Fleximum" refers to mothers who work (mainly part-time) and who are similarly part-time mothers. They are generally a combination of "Organisers" and "Huggers". Approximately half of all British mothers belong to this group. The Fleximum might switch between being at home and putting in a baby into a nursery, creating confusion in the child.

Oliver James' central message, however, is that 90% of nurseries provide either poor or else insufficiently good childcare. Also far too many children under the age of three are shoved into nursery at an age where they're simply unready either to cope without their mother or to play with other children without conflicts and confrontation. This tends to lead to increased stress (cortisol) levels for the child and can contribute to aggression in later life.

In the UK around 13% of mothers are reckoned to develop depression during pregnancy or after the birth. (Probably the real number is higher, as postnatal depression often goes undiagnosed.) Important precipitating internal factors can be financial stress, feeling helpless, nerves about not be able to cope with the baby, while external factors include divorce, an absent partner, a death in family, work worries or simply having too many children to cope with.

Interestingly approximately 20% of babies develop colic and (for that reason) cry extensively, something that can naturally contributes to depression in their mothers.

And yet, I'm still asked: What constitutes depression? Professor Paul Gilbert describes depression as a cycle of bad thoughts such as (but not necessarily including) "I'm worthless" or "I'm useless" or "Everything is hopeless" in a constant circle of anxious thoughts. These thoughts hold the depressed person in an iron grip.

It is not hard to see how induced thoughts like these might originate from another person—and that a person constantly inducing such thoughts might well be a narcissist. For the depressed person (or his victim) life can become an endless struggle with thoughts of worthlessness and uselessness constantly circling in the depressed person's brain. Some elements of psychological thinking take the view that such depressed thoughts can emerge from out of nowhere but that when circumstances change for the worse (like unemployment, financial difficulties, bereavement etc.) then latent depression hits with full force.

Psychology has yet to make the connection between the depressed victim and his/her accompanying narcissist, someone who constantly needs to push down his victims. The out-of-the-blue depression so often discussed in psychology is something that Oliver James and many others remain unconvinced by. One starting point for future psychotherapy will be when such depression is considered rare, and when mostly those with a narcissistic parent or partner will be treated for depression.

Regarding nurture or nature for children's development then Oliver James is firmly in the nurture camp, believing that if only genes mattered then children could be put into any nursery or go into any school because their environment would make no discernible difference. Personally I not only support the nurture camp but hope to demonstrate why so many scientists have miscalculated its importance.

Firstly (as Oliver James points out) higher cortisol levels in mothers will assuredly be passed on through the placenta to the fetus. Thus even as a newborn, the baby can have slightly elevated cortisol levels.

Related to this, a mother with postnatal depression will not be able to care and relate to her child emotionally, contributing not only to higher stress levels in the child but also to higher levels of cortisol inside the baby.

Thirdly, a baby put into day-care too early is also at risk of yet higher level of cortisol (leading to a more aggressive adult later on in life).

Of course, such babies can—years later—wind up in therapy. Oliver James is critical of Cognitive Behaviour Therapy (CBT) because it fails to focus on the patient's relationship to his parents: instead he recommends psychoanalytic treatment over a minimum of three years.

Fascinatingly, Oliver James recommends that these three questions be put to a psychotherapist before embarking on such psychotherapy:

1) "Are you aware that the latest evidence shows that depression is less influenced by genetic factors than by the care a person received early in life?"

2) "Are you familiar with Attachment Theory, and is it help with my attachment that you will provide?"

3) "Will you focus primarily on the way my childhood is causing my depression?"

It is his contention that the answers to these should enable the potential analysand to make a good choice of analyst.

In Susan Jeffers' book Feel The Fear And Do It Anyway: How to Turn Your Fear and Indecision into Confidence and Action, she brings up the important point that women with dominant parents (or parent) can find an abusive relationship completely normal and even natural (the "compliant victims").

In Claire Golomb's book Trapped in the Mirror she opines that the main reason for narcissism is having a narcissistic mother. There is an element of truth here, but the numbers don't add up, because if approximately 10% of the general population is on the narcissistic spectrum, then every narcissistic woman would have to give birth to four children, where in reality many women never have children at all, and the overall birth rate in the UK is well below 2% (and the UK's birthrate is higher than the European average).

All of these authors and psychologists have something important to say, Oliver James in particular. In my final chapter, I hope to summarise my own thinking on the subject.

Arnoldology: Summary And Overview

The core of this book is that it is primarily mothers suffering postnatal depression who create monstrous narcissists like Adolf Hitler. What do we call a new theory about Adolf Hitler, WWII and something that affects our world?

"The General Theory of Postnatal Depression and Narcissism" is a bit long-winded. Then of course it could be Hitlerology: I can't help thinking that it would be good to finally get something useful out of Hitler, after all the death, misery and destruction he wrought on the world. But anything mentioning Hitler can understandably influence some people adversely.

Therefore I recommend the neutral Arnoldology.

What Arnoldology does is to seek out the connection between postnatal depression (resulting in narcissism) and a whole range of human suffering, from school bullying and Internet stalking, all the way up to war-mongering and kick-starting the Holocaust. The connection between mother and baby, in the first three years of life, is absolutely key as to whether that child will grow up able to relate to others—or whether lack of maternal responsiveness can lead, from innocently tipping over a cup of milk, to growing up to invade Poland.

The key is emotional affirmation. Even a negative reaction is better than no reaction at all, thus the incipient narcissist learns to hungrily feed off of the thrill of causing despair. This not only can but inevitably will become a lifelong addiction, incurable by anything that we know about today. The brain connections required for normality aren't possible later, if they aren't formed early enough. This is also the clue to the lack of remorse in those affected. Horrible as it sounds, they literally can't care.

I personally believe that, as a consequence, a narcissist should not be allowed to hold high political office, or to work as a psychiatrist, doctor or CEO. Their potential for destruction is simply too high to take the risk (and yes, there are tests available today to differentiate between a true narcissist and a person of strong ambition. Dr Hare has done one, and other experts have as well.)

And I believe that the school bully, conman, and cyberstalker all the way to mass-murdering dictators such as Hitler, Stalin, Mao, Saddam Hussein and Gaddafi have something in common: they never learned to relate emotionally to their mothers; and thus from an early age developed the ability to fish for weaknesses in their victims and to find ways to break them down. The methods used by the narcissist might be well documented in literature and movie films, but as far as I know the causes and origin apart from the vague "all in the genes" theory has never before been published.

Arnoldology accepted, we can begin to comprehend some of our cultural past in a different light. For example, the penalty of crucifixion—standard practice during the Roman period—would have been heaven for early narcissists in the Roman Empire. (It normally took three days for victims to slowly suffocate on the cross.) Their gladiatorial games also pandered to the narcissistic mind.

What would be horrific to a normal person—wild animals tearing fellow humans into bloody pulp, armed men "fighting" unarmed men, screams of despair from the victims of the "games"—what more could someone like Caligula dream of? I even believe that one of the motivations for the all-conquering Roman Empire was to create despair in whole peoples—and that the gladiatorial "games" were dreamed up in order to create artificial suffering when there were fewer countries to conquer.

Every now and then the Romans assassinated their own emperors, including Caesar and Nero, whether for political advantage or when they felt that their cruelty and power went too far. It's not hard to draw a parallel to all the assassinations attempt aimed at Adolf Hitler, once it became obvious that Hitler not only created misery and despair in Germany's neighbouring countries, but also in Germany itself. The assassins would probably be far less sickeningly narcissistic—or in other words, more nearly-normal people who had had enough of watching other's despair.

And it's not only these historical events that are explained by my theory. What are the odds that the Crusades, the Spanish Inquisition, the witch hunts in early Massachusetts, the slave trade and the French Revolution were spawned, encouraged and enacted by the kind of narcissists that Hitler would gladly have welcomed to the Eagle's Nest?

We have already mentioned Stalin's starved and brutalised Soviet Union, Mao's induced famine and forced labour camps, Adolf Hitler's Holocaust and Saddam Hussein's chemical warfare against his own people. I suspect that the Khmer Rouge reign of terror, ethnic "cleansing" in Ruanda and Bosnia, and the simmering conflict between Arab and Israeli all have the same root cause.

Words such as truth and falsehood, good and evil, right and wrong and indeed morality itself hold no meaning for the narcissist. Despite their fascination for the rest of us, the approximate 10% of the population to whom perhaps they ought most to concern are tone-deaf to them. In the view of anyone on the narcissistic spectrum any notion of morality becomes a curiosity at best.

In short, philosophy has tried to posit timeless and universal truths without considering that part of the population are clinically without conscience and are therefore so far outside the sphere of "right and wrong" that many philosophical arguments are incomprehensible to them.

There is endless documentation about serial killers like Ted Bundy, but there is almost always a complete lack of attention to their earliest years. If one is interested (a big "if") one can learn about their school misdeeds, their allies or their lack of them, their schemes of infamy, and all about the blood—but about the fertile earth from which their narcissism sprang, hardly a word.

Social deprivation is by no means the complete story in creating murderers: there are endless examples of children from poor and deprived areas with completely healthy mothers who grow up well and never harm anybody, while Bin Laden was the son of a Saudi billionaire. In short, family background is a poor indicator of where the next mass murderer is coming from. Robert Hare reckons up to 40% of top-level corporate executives are narcissistic, and, as the old joke goes, it can be more dangerous to walk around with your wallet visible in a wealthy neighbourhood than in a bad neighborhood. (In a poor neighborhood the narcissists steal your wallet: in a wealthy neighbourhood they steal your pension or your savings.)

In short, the best method of crime prevention we could do (and I admit that it doesn't sound glamorous) is to ensure that all mothers are given the support they need after giving birth and for the three years that follow. Midwives need to be trained to recognise the earliest signs of depression: more antidepressants will probably be needed (which may in turn affect breast-feeding and other issues).

It is a well established fact that re-offending rate is very high in practically every country in the world: something that some right-wing people grumble is because prisons are "too comfortable". I have no opinion on the luxuriousness of prisons—which must anyway vary from country to country. I simply wish to observe that one reason for the high rate of recidivism could simply be that narcissists, sociopaths and psychopaths simply love what they do, and that and it gives them an enormous narcissistic "kick" to see the despair in their victims' faces. This notion that a thief only steals because he had a deprived childhood is an incorrect but comforting illusion for many well-meaning social workers.

Also, this theory (that social deprivation in childhood would create crime) does not in any way explain white-collar crime, which arguably impacts on far more people than violent crime (as well as being hugely under-reported).

A great deal of crime has simply moved into the internet, especially since anybody (poor or rich) can for very little cash get hold of a second-hand laptop. So while a couple of shoplifters might be pursued by film crews in siren-screeching police cars, the internet hacker who gets access to our bank accounts and credit card details usually goes undetected and unpunished.

In short, normal people choose to work at a job while the narcissist chooses to specialise in crime, at least partly because it gives them a narcissistic thrill to steal money from people. (Anyone clever enough to hack in and steal money over the internet is surely smart enough to hold down any computer job—but that wouldn't create the same narcissistic joy.) So crime has very little to do with poverty, except in that it can of course be depressing to be poor.

Arnoldology is a new way to look at the world, establishing those on the narcissistic spectrum as driving forces in the world (and incidentally addressing related shortcomings in history, psychology, philosophy, business, economics, politics and criminology). Old ways of explaining world conflicts including capitalism, socialism, communism, dictatorships, corporate monopolies and religious tension must be re-assessed in the light of Arnoldology, which posits that they are merely tools for narcissists to use in order to reach their warped and twisted goals.

Some people would say that places like Northern Ireland (not to mention Israel and Palestine) are simply places where any number of generations remain politically obdurate. Instead, I would suggest that such places are narcissistic paradises pure and simple—places where narcissists can for historical reasons easily find and feed off their prey.

This comparison might be clarified when we look at Germany (specifically from 1914 to 1945) in rather greater detail. By understanding Germany—and Hitler—during this period we should absorb the truth that only in Germany was the population ripe for narcissism to conquer a high enough percentage of the younger population in order to enable Hitler to gain power, thus dismantling any form of democracy.

Yet if we consider Hitler as what passes for a "normal" narcissist, then he certainly did what narcissists normally do: in other words, he seized power, suppressed opposition and created a state based of fear (in fact a narcissistic paradise) whereby the Gestapo endlessly invented new "enemies" to satisfy his sick tastes.

We can still wonder how that could be allowed to happen. History assures us that it was the overly-harsh peace deal of 1918 (plus Nazi propaganda) that tricked ordinary Germans into voting for the Nazis. However, just recall that Hitler was assuredly not the only German narcissist in the 1910s and 1920s. Then imagine that perhaps not only the customary 10% of the German population was narcissistic (or worse) but that the numbers might have reached as high as 40%, thanks to unspeakable levels of inflation and the torture of bereavement and defeat.

Under these circumstances we have an utterly different explanation of WWII: one that completely overturns all historical explanations. This was one of the starting points of this book, to upend explanations regarding WWII, words like evil in philosophy, notions including crime in criminology—not to mention the reason why international accountants constantly "get it wrong".

And they're not the only experts who can get things wrong. Every Spring for over forty years I believed that I caught a germ resulting in sinus or occasionally bronchitis—often several times a season. If I went to a doctor and got penicillin I'd be well after seven days, otherwise my cold would linger on for weeks, if not for months. We've all heard how Vitamin C can help a cold so I used to drink lots and lots of orange juice. In fact, vitamins, cough medicine, water steam, woolly hats: you name it, I tried it. In every school photo I had a cold sore on my lips, while doctor after doctor told me, "Lots of people get colds in the Spring." I became resigned, and thought that this was simply how my life would always be.

This I believed for over forty years, until I went on vacation to Spain and enjoyed fresh-squeezed orange juice. My lips flared up with blisters and (since nobody I travelled with had a cold) the idea dawned on me that perhaps, just perhaps, I was allergic to oranges! So I just simply stopped drinking orange juice and I have not had a single cold sore since. Now it is clear that colds are big business for pharmaceuticals companies and I sometimes wonder how many colds are actually allergies (in my case, almost 95%). I suspect that a general allergy test could save billions for the NHS.

Eventually I had several allergy tests done through the excellent Medical Doctor in London and it turned out that I am allergic to birch pollen, hazelnuts and oranges, and after getting desensitization injections from a specialist at King's College Hospital I now enjoy a cold-free Spring every year. We can only speculate as to how many people (especially now allergies are so much more common) might be in the same position.

This is an illustration and not as off-topic as it might seem, as to how so many well-meaning people can get their thinking wrong for decades (even for centuries). However, when it comes to narcissism, sociopathy and psychopathy I think that mistakes are of truly critical importance.

Narcissism, sociopaths and psychopathy are primarily caused by mothers with postnatal depression. Society at large could save billions of pounds (and any number of lives) by understanding and recognising this, doing something about it and thus giving us a world with less fraud, crime and misery in it. That is my hope and intention in writing this book—although I doubt that this will happen during my lifetime or for many generations. Perhaps in several centuries we will move towards a world where respect for individuals will be the norm. However, my understanding in 2013 is that the vast majority of postnatal depression goes undiagnosed, untreated or even both. We are thus storing up trouble in the form of narcissists, sociopaths and psychopaths for decade after decade, even century after century, to come.

History, psychology, economics, business, criminology and philosophy all attempt to deal with the narcissistic spectrum and yet still attempt to explain (as best they can) world events as if they were occasioned by normal people. This I believe is a major flaw in such subjects today.

This is a book about narcissism, the most deviant and widespread personality disorder filtering throughout our society—and one strikingly hard to identify unless you know exactly what to look for. Narcissism surfaces first at home as a toddler and becomes clearer at school. The school bully is inevitably a narcissist, for whom bullying serves a particular need. The goal for the bullying narcissist is not merely to tease but rather to create despair—indeed, thoroughly breaking the other child down. Whether the methods used are mental or physical (for example, to beat up the victim, or to lead a mob to do so) the ultimate goal is to drive another child into complete despair.

A person who teases others but who is in no way a narcissist will know where the boundaries fall between teasing and bullying: a narcissist, however, has quite another agenda. For the narcissist, bullying is simply another tool for getting what he most craves: his victim's despair. The notion that we are "all good people" and that only a few "bad eggs" end up in prison can no longer be part of an overall understanding of humanity.

With this in mind we urgently need to understand why some people become narcissists, while others don't, since this knowledge will not only affect our view of WWII but also of other historical events (for example: the Russian revolution, the French revolution, and the Khmer Rouge, to mention just a few).

Also, even if it escapes immediate investigation in this book, psychology, philosophy, criminology, business administration and even economics stand on very shaky ground once the true nature of narcissism and its effects on society becomes more widely known. (Imagine explaining crime, financial crises and recent corporate crashes as nothing more than the obvious outcome of narcissistic behaviour. The topic is simply too wide-ranging: despite my best efforts it will have to be put off to later publications.)

Tragically, no psychotherapy in the world can change this story. It is common knowledge that narcissists (sociopaths or psychopaths) can suddenly, out of the blue, apparently develop schizophrenia or other persuasive psychoses—and yet, after having been referred to a more relaxed mental hospital, recover with surprising suddenness, only to be released again into society. (Remember, most narcissists are never jailed. Instead we meet them almost every day in society at large, where they often hold high-status jobs.)

By understanding how people become narcissists post-babyhood we might one day be able to do something about the problem, producing a far more loving and productive world: one which wastes far less money on prisons, police and the military, and one where fraud, crime (and even murder) become far less common.

This is of course a Utopian vision. In real life, narcissism is as much part of our surroundings as rain, lightning, cloud formations, erosion, corporative crashes or depressive illness itself. It's a never-ending cycle, where one generation after another can rush to war with each other, while no generation learns from previous generations' mistakes.

When we look at military conflicts around the world then it isn't hard to see that narcissism is the main driving factor. We have already seen how WWII was actually impelled forward by narcissism, in its case created by hardship of losing WWI, German hyperinflation, plus multiple bereavements (dead husbands, fathers and brothers). The economic depression that followed made Germany the worst affected country in the world, even before the stockmarket crash of 1929.

It's no accident that, out of all the countries in the world, Al-Qaeda found its support base in Afghanistan, basically choosing to take over the country because it had suffered horrifically during the Soviet occupation, creating the ideal narcissistic foundation for a terrorist group. (The irony is that it was USA that supported the Afghans in the war against the Soviet Union, whereupon Al Qaeda turned viciously against the USA.)

Just as Hitler and the Nazis could seamlessly move from fighting Communists, Socialists, intellectuals and eventually in 1938 turn against the Jews, Al-Qaeda moved from fighting the Soviet Union to turn on their own backers, the USA. In terms of logic all this makes no sense at all but from a narcissistic point of view it make perfect sense, in the constant search for new narcissistic victims. Narcissism has its own logic, something that I term "narcissistic logic" in that it has small enough connection to what is generally known as logic. In fact, "narcissistic logic" as we've already seen, serves a specific purpose to the narcissist, inexplicable by any kind of previously codified logic.

Looking back in history we can see outstanding conflicts between, for example, Catholics and Protestants, communism and capitalism, Muslims and Christians. With reference to my own philosophy, all those ways of looking at conflicts can be declared obsolete because narcissism can explain any type of conflict.

In short, it's personal. Individual narcissists shove their way to power, and then inevitably do what they always do. When this is fully understood then historical analysis becomes obsolete because it doesn't matter what a narcissist say when using his bizarre "narcissistic logic" to explain why they started the war, because in the end it's only narcissistic need that determines what actually happens. Narcissistic logic is not burdened by proofs: instead, narcissists use it to express whatever suits their purpose best.

As for anybody who tries to find any kind of logic in "narcissistic logic", I'm afraid he will be deeply disappointed. "Narcissistic logic" is really exclusively beneficial to a narcissist, in order for him or her to excuse the inexcusable. From a philosophical point of view it is as best rubbish and at worst false, yet still our media uncritically regurgitates plenty of narcissistic "reasoning" in our daily life.

In terms of economics any number of toothless American Presidents have feared to follow the example of splitting up Standard Oil in the 1940s into what nowadays are BP, Gulf Oil, Standard Oil, Chevron, Royal Dutch Shell, Esso and ExxonMobil. It's monopolies that prevent development, cementing the business world into slower growth. (And only from a "narcissistic logic" point of view do monopolies makes any kind of sense.)

That corporations like Microsoft and Oracle continue to control their market niche to a far greater degree than Standard Oil ever did has not succeeded in winning the argument. President Bill Clinton started the process of analyzing how to split up Microsoft—but President George Bush, backed by Microsoft donations, closed down the process with the reasoning that "they need peace to work".

In fact, what we see in the USA today is not real capitalism but rather monopolies defending themselves from outside competition. The list of corporations that are realistically only monopolies in disguise grows ever longer, but the topic is just too huge for this book. Someday we will study the true nature of corporate, governments and banking's "narcissistic logic" in great detail, but that is for the future and not the present.

So, what is Arnoldology? Arnoldology is a theory, but at the same time more than a theory. It's a new tool for understanding. It's a new way to look at the world as it is, and narcissism for what it is. After finishing this book you will better understand that there is only one conflict in the world, the one between the narcissists and the rest of us.

In fact, this short but immensely ambitious book will alter your perspective forever.

Appendix 1: Why Many Narcissistic And Psychopatic "Twin Studies" Remain A Waste Of Time

The second part of the documentary mentioned earlier ("Help me love my baby") is all about a mother called Sophie, and one of her twin daughters, Grace.

Here we see a mother with postnatal depression able to relate completely normally to one of her identical twin daughters but not to the other! Years later, a psychiatric expert is astonished to discover that one twin is normal while the other is a narcissist—and all because their mother could love one twin but not the other. One can only conclude that any psychologically-based study of identical twins (so often used as comparisons) might prove similarly irrelevant.

This will probably come as a shock for those scientists studying identical twins, at least with regard to whether or not narcissism or psychopathy might be genetically carried. Clearly they are not if you (like me) believe that the mother's postnatal depression is the main cause. However, one major contribution to DNA theory criticism regarding twins is psychologist Jay Joseph's The Missing Gene and The Gene Illusion. Joseph's criticisms range from the selection of twins to the misinterpretation of data. As far as I can observe he never considered that a mother with postnatal depression might be able to love one identical twin but not the other; and that this fact makes any form of mental health study during the past century involving identical twins at best incomplete.

His criticism regarding twin studies was with regard to schizophrenia, criminal behavior, IQ-levels, mental disorders, autism, attention-deficit hyperactivity disorder, schizophrenia and bipolar disorder. He has worked with the equally highly-respected Oliver James, yet I believe that they missed my crucial point, which opens the door for a completely new interpretation of identical twin studies in the future. But that is one of the beauties of science, which is always moving forward and reassessing previous theories in the light of new evidence!

Appendix 2 Case 5 - The Yorkshire Ripper

In one sense, Peter Sutcliffe was caught with his trousers down. "The Yorkshire Ripper" was arrested for a minor traffic offense. At the police station he was asked to remove his trench coat. To the astonishment of the police he was wearing trousers in which he had cut a hole for easy access to his genitals and added cosy padding on his knees, to enable himself to masturbate more comfortably next to the next victim he had hammered to death. Now the Yorkshire police certainly failed to cover themselves with glory with regard to catching the Ripper—they had interviewed Sutcliffe on three separate occasions before—but it was the customized trousers that finally got their interest.

Sutcliffe was convicted of killing thirteen women and attempting to murder seven others, but he probably killed still more, as his victims were mainly prostitutes and thus not necessarily on society's radar. What Sutcliffe did was to sneak up on his victims and hit them from behind with a hammer. I believe that he aimed in such a way so that they wouldn't immediately be killed but would instead turn around, possibly even pleading for their lives, so Sutcliffe would be able to relish their despair. Then Sutcliffe could open his trench coat and masturbate from all the narcissistic excitement of his own "power" (he might even have done this as his victim died).

Later on Sutcliffe claimed that he heard a voice from God ordering him to kill those women, but it doesn't require great genius to pretend to madness once caught red-handed. Many people consider Peter Sutcliffe complicated and mysterious, but actually he's simply a common narcissist, with a little sexual twist. Had he been given psychotherapy at a younger age he could have learned more manipulative skills and possibly charmed himself into women's houses and killed them more privately, but that's all that psychoanalysis could have done for him.

Appendix 3 Tv And Film Violence

There is an almost an endless debate regarding the influence of film (and TV) violence on young people: whether it can lead to "copy-cat" crimes, or de-sensitize the vulnerable. I believe that the question is wrongly put. A more useful question would ask if such violence can inspire narcissistic people towards crime and bullying: and the answer to that is no doubt positive.

The rest of us are capable of differentiating sensibly between make-believe and reality.

Appendix 4- The Narcissistic Cowboy Builder

Police put warnings through our doors, it constantly surfaces on consumer programmes, and we occasionally hear rumours about it locally: the cowboy builder who pushes his way into the houses of the elderly or gullible, talking persuasively about new windows, kitchens or extensions. Surprisingly enough, they always insist on being paid the whole (or near it) before work commences. Then after weeks (even months) of creating either nothing or else mere chaos disappears with the money.

You may think: from Hitler to a mere rip-off artist? Where's the connection? The connection is narcissism—and malignancy. This is no normal builder, a guy like you and me trying as best he can to make a living. This is someone who routinely, day after day, year after year, attempts to swindle people out of their money, leaving as much anguish and mess as possible in his wake. Of course, it's not an international level (Hitler) or in involving fantastic sums of money (Enron)—but the lure of doing it is, on its smaller scale, identical. In the end the victim might be left without a wall (or even a roof), or just with everything upset and nothing done except the theft of plenty of money.

True: nobody dies, but this kind of builder remains on the narcissistic spectrum: the kind of person who thrills to getting phone calls from clients deep in incoherent fury or desperation. It gives the cowboy builder an enormous narcissistic power boost to hear a client testify to their frustration and suffering.

The notion that the cowboy builder made a mistake, miscalculated or isn't aware of exactly what they're doing is pure nonsense. Some persist in this "career" throughout their whole working life!—bankrupting one "company" only to start up another—or else having no company basis at all beyond the ability to take vulnerable people in.

For normal people this kind of attitude remains impossible to understand and many—even most—clients apparently attempt to appeal to the cowboy builders' conscience (non-existent), good citizenship (ditto) or even love for mankind (don't make me laugh). In fact the cowboy builder is just a normal narcissist, sociopath or psychopath, and victimizing others is simply makes them feel clever and powerful.

When giving evidence in court they normally try to deny it all, claiming that they're perfectly honest and that it was only unfortunate circumstances and bad luck behind the case, but this is merely self-preservation. In truth, no numbers of years in jail, punitive fines or public embarrassment would make any difference because the sheer narcissistic joy of having ruined somebody's property and to hear their victim's pleading with them over and over again to fix everything is irresistible to someone of this mentality.

Even in 2013 it is hard for most people to understand that 10% of the population aren't like us and never ever can be. They can never feel remorse, though they <u>can</u> be extremely good in pretending remorse when the justice system might reward remorse in exchange for a more lenient prison term. Then, the narcissist will perform better than a professional Shakespearean, and many watching (sometimes even the victim) might even believe that such remorse is real.

Remember: a genuine narcissist can feel <u>nothing</u> for their victims: indeed, and a confrontation with a past victim can only afford a narcissist an extra joy, as something they can relish and even feed off privately afterwards.

Short Summary

In this book Hans Arnold demonstrates how postnatal depression in the mother can create both narcissists and psychopaths. Using examples of famous serial killers and mass murderers, he demonstrates beyond reasonable doubt that, in each case, the mother's depression had a powerfully adverse effect on the child. For example, Hitler's mother lost two children to diphtheria 18 and 15 months before Adolf was born—and another died of measles when Adolf was only eight months. Hans Arnold analyzes Hitler's narcissism in the light of his mother's own suffering.

Put briefly, in order to get any emotional response at all from his mother Adolf developed a "narcissistic game" in order to shock his mother into at least some reaction, even if it was only an expression of despair. The youthful narcissist eventually became "hooked" on sensation, seeking more and more extreme reactions—not only from his mother or caregiver, but from whatever victim he could find. What was true for Adolf Hitler is unluckily also true for every child whose mother suffers from postnatal depression, even today.

Using examples from history as well as serial killings as recent as Anders Breivik's Norway shootings, Arnold demonstrates how postnatal depression-induced narcissism is behind events from internet bullying to modern terrorism, opening up new perspectives on history, psychology, criminology, and corporate ethics.

Arnold makes connections never before attempted. After finishing this book you will understand that there is only one conflict in the world, the one between the narcissists and the rest of us.

This short but immensely ambitious book will alter your perspective forever.

Printed in Great Britain
by Amazon.co.uk, Ltd.,
Marston Gate.